PHP Team Development

Easy and effective team work using MVC, agile
development, source control, testing, bug tracking,
and more

Samisa Abeysinghe

PUBLISHING

BIRMINGHAM - MUMBAI

PHP Team Development

First published: September 2009

Production Reference: 1240809

Published by Packt Publishing Ltd.
32 Lincoln Road
Olton
Birmingham, B27 6PA, UK.

ISBN 978-1-847195-06-7

www.packtpub.com

Cover Image by Ed Maclean (edmaclean@gmail.com)

Credits

Author
Samisa Abeysinghe

Reviewers
Deepak Vohra

Garvin Hicking

Acquisition Editor
Sarah Cullington

Development Editor
Dilip Venkatesh

Technical Editors
Mehul Shetty

Akash Johari

Copy Editor
Leonard D'Silva

Indexer
Monica Ajmera

Editorial Team Leader
Akshara Aware

Project Team Leader
Lata Basantani

Project Coordinator
Rajashree Hamine

Proofreader
Joel T. Johnson

Production Coordinator
Adline Swetha Jesuthas

Cover Work
Adline Swetha Jesuthas

Drawing Coordinator
Nilesh R. Mohite

About the Author

Samisa Abeysinghe has nearly ten years of industrial experience with various software projects. He has been an Apache committer for many years and has worked for software product companies as well as software services companies.

Samisa was the project leader for WSO2 Web services Framework for PHP projects for a couple of years and has an in-depth understanding on the enterprise use of PHP. He has been involved in helping many project teams use WSO2 WSF/PHP for enterprise projects.

As director of engineering at WSO2, Samisa now looks after multiple teams working on various projects on a daily basis and gets involved with defining and fine-tuning processes and practices to ensure a project's success.

Samisa is also the author of the book RESTful PHP Web Services.

I would like to thank all the people who have worked with me on software projects from the day I started working in the software industry. All those people have greatly helped me in understanding this complex domain.

I would like to mention the WSO2 team, including Sanjiva Weerewarana-CEO, and Paul Fremantle-CTO, all the members of the engineering leadership, as well as all the engineers. While it has been a pleasure to work with such a skilled team, it has also helped me to understand the software engineering realities better in practice.

I would also like to mention the great helping hands rendered by the technical reviewers of this book as well as the project coordinator of this book.

About the Reviewers

Deepak Vohra is a consultant and a principal member of the NuBean.com software company. He is a Sun Certified Java Programmer and Web Component Developer, and has worked in the fields of XML, Java programming and J2EE for over five years. He is the co-author of the Apress book Pro XML Development with Java Technology and was the technical reviewer for the O'Reilly book *WebLogic: The Definitive Guide*. He was also the technical reviewer for the Course Technology PTR book *Ruby Programming for the Absolute Beginner*, and the technical editor for the Manning Publications book *Prototype and Scriptaculous in Action*. Deepak is also the author of the Packt Publishing books JDBC 4.0 and Oracle JDeveloper for J2EE Development, and Processing XML Documents with Oracle JDeveloper 11g.

Garvin Hicking is a passionate web-developer, who is engaged in open source projects like Serendipity (Lead Developer) and phpMyAdmin. He works at the Internet agency Faktor E GmbH in Bonn (Germany). Being up-to-date, he has been involved in writing or reviewing several books about PHP, the most recent one being the official documentation of the PHP-Blog application Serendipity. Aside from his professional work, he and his girlfriend enjoy taking professional photographs.

Table of Contents

Preface

This book is about ensuring project success for PHP teams. It explores technical as well as non technical aspects that matter when achieving project success. On the technical front, designing to divide complexity to conquer complex problems, keeping things simple in the design, choosing the right process, and monitoring and improving the process are important aspects. On the non technical front, making sure that they collaborate effectively, the team should be open to changes. The team should be open to user feedback. Having the right mindset about quality and other aspects related to project success are discussed.

What this book covers

Chapter 1, Software is Complex, explains the complexities that we face while working with today's software projects. PHP projects, some years ago, used to be small projects involving one or two people. However, today, we need teams of people for PHP projects. This chapter explores the need for teams for PHP projects. It also discusses how software engineering principles help with PHP projects. There is an increasing need to use a process for PHP projects. The complexity of having a team is figuring out how to divide the project's problem among team members and solve it. This chapter discusses how to divide and conquer projects. We will discuss how patterns help the PHP project to cope with complexity. Finally, we will explore how to use tools to manage the development and collaboration within the PHP team.

Chapter 2, MVC and Software Teams, discusses the MVC pattern in depth and how MVC can help in a PHP project. It also explores how to use the MVC pattern as the guiding principle to break down the complexity of a project, and how to implement MVC with a team. It also discusses the integration challenges that are faced in putting together all the pieces of MVC that are developed by different team members.

Chapter 3, Dealing with Complexity, discusses in depth how we can make use of software design patterns to cope with complexities in a software project. We will also discuss how PHP MVC frameworks simplify the complexity of a project. When using a PHP framework, there are a bunch of expectations; we will explore what to expect and what to look for in a PHP framework. The mere use of a PHP framework would not guarantee project success. Hence, we will discuss how to achieve team success with PHP frameworks in this chapter. We will also look at some leading PHP frameworks. Moreover, we will also learn how to make things simple while using a PHP framework.

Chapter 4, The Process Matters, explains the relationship between the process and the product. We will discuss, in depth, the consequences of ignoring the process and why the process must be respected. We will learn how to move from no process to having a process. We will explore the motivation that is required for a process, how a process helps, and does not hinder a PHP project. We will also study a simple process model that can be used for PHP projects.

Chapter 5, Agile Works Best, will introduce agile philosophy, including agile values and agile principles. We will discuss common problems and fears that developers face when developing a product, and see how agility can help to overcome them. We will discuss extreme programming principles, and also learn the advantages of agile process models. Finally, we will explore how we can achieve team agility.

Chapter 6, Ways of Collaboration, discusses the challenges faced while working with teams, and we explore the implications of assumptions made by team members. Then we will learn collaboration techniques for ensuring seamless integration of the various components and layers developed by the team members. We will dig into the details of source control, bug control, and configuration management, and learn how those relate to effective team collaboration. Moreover, we will discuss some tools that we can use for communication and collaboration.

Chapter 7, Continuous Improvement, will explain how to deal with change in PHP applications. In order to make sure the software that we develop is useful, we have to make sure that we are willing to embrace change and also be ready to evolve the system, as we move along. We also have to ensue that the process being used is effective. We will discuss how we can evolve the PHP application and also measure the effectiveness of our process. People development is also another important aspect of continuous improvement when ensuring success with teams. We will learn the team management and people development aspect in this chapter.

What you need for this book

This book does not assume any prerequisites. If you have worked with a project team on a PHP application, it will make it easier to relate to your experiences. However, if you are a beginner, and want to learn what it takes to work with a team and be successful, this book will provide a wealth of knowledge.

Who this book is for

This book is for PHP developers who work in complex PHP projects. Those who want to know the secrets of success for PHP projects that meet the complex demands of today's enterprise can benefit from this book.

This book can also be useful for project managers who are looking to be successful with PHP projects.

Those who are acting as stakeholders of PHP projects, such as clients, or those who want to sponsor PHP projects, can also learn what to expect and how to deal with PHP project team with this book.

Conventions

In this book, you will find a number of styles of text that distinguish between different kinds of information. Here are some examples of these styles, and an explanation of their meaning.

New terms and **important words** are shown in bold. Words that you see on the screen, in menus or dialog boxes for example, appear in the text like this: "Once a developer starts working on the issue, the issue will transit to **In-progress** state".

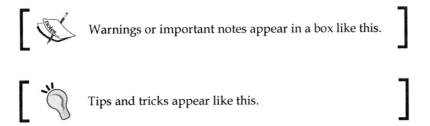

Warnings or important notes appear in a box like this.

Tips and tricks appear like this.

Reader feedback

Feedback from our readers is always welcome. Let us know what you think about this book—what you liked or may have disliked. Reader feedback is important for us to develop titles that you really get the most out of.

To send us general feedback, simply send an email to feedback@packtpub.com, and mention the book title via the subject of your message.

If there is a book that you need and would like to see us publish, please send us a note in the **SUGGEST A TITLE** form on www.packtpub.com or email suggest@packtpub.com.

If there is a topic that you have expertise in and you are interested in either writing or contributing to a book on, see our author guide on www.packtpub.com/authors.

Customer support

Now that you are the proud owner of a Packt book, we have a number of things to help you to get the most from your purchase.

Downloading the example code for the book

Visit http://www.packtpub.com/files/code/7542_Code.zip to directly download the example code.

The downloadable files contain instructions on how to use them.

Errata

Although we have taken every care to ensure the accuracy of our content, mistakes do happen. If you find a mistake in one of our books—maybe a mistake in the text or the code—we would be grateful if you would report this to us. By doing so, you can save other readers from frustration, and help us to improve subsequent versions of this book. If you find any errata, please report them by visiting http://www.packtpub.com/support, selecting your book, clicking on the **let us know** link, and entering the details of your errata. Once your errata are verified, your submission will be accepted and the errata added to any list of existing errata. Any existing errata can be viewed by selecting your title from http://www.packtpub.com/support.

Piracy

Piracy of copyright material on the Internet is an ongoing problem across all media. At Packt, we take the protection of our copyright and licenses very seriously. If you come across any illegal copies of our works, in any form, on the Internet, please provide us with the location address or web site name immediately so that we can pursue a remedy.

Please contact us at copyright@packtpub.com with a link to the suspected pirated material.

We appreciate your help in protecting our authors, and our ability to bring you valuable content.

Questions

You can contact us at questions@packtpub.com if you are having a problem with any aspect of the book, and we will do our best to address it.

)

1
Software is Complex

Useful software evolves over time in order to adapt to the ever changing environment and to cope with the ever increasing demands in the real world. Therefore, useful software becomes increasingly complex over time. This phenomenon applies to PHP applications as well.

During the early days of PHP, the systems written were fairly simple and straightforward. In fact, when Rasmus Lerdorf first developed PHP, the objective was very simple—'Make my life easy with dynamic web applications'. It was a one person effort to start with. Over a period of time, more and more individuals got interested in PHP and used it for their own web applications. Their applications were simple, hardly exceeding 100 PHP scripts and, more often than not, managed by a single person.

As more people gained interest in PHP, for its simplicity and ease of use, the number of use cases increased. This resulted in people wanting to do more with PHP, especially with the rise of the Internet and enterprises looking into using Internet for business applications. The Novel Applications of the Web 2.0 era also increased the demand for rich applications on the Web, along with the need for powerful programming options.

PHP, as a scripting language, has evolved remarkably to meet up to the new requirements. Therefore, as we all know, PHP became the language of choice for the majority of complex and interesting applications that are deployed on the Internet today.

If you look around the Web, some of the most used applications such as Flickr (http://www.flickr.com/) and Facebook (http://www.facebook.com/) are PHP-based. Any web hosting solution that is found around the Web today provides support for PHP. Drupal (http://drupal.org/), Joomla (http://www.joomla.org/), and WordPress (http://wordpress.org/), the popular content management systems that are deployed by millions, are all PHP-based.

As the adoption of PHP becomes wider and the use becomes broader, the feature set and tools continue to expand. At the same time, organizations tend to choose PHP as the language of choice for complex web applications, because it is battle tested, hardened over time, and proven to work. Thus, the chances of the software project you are involved with being PHP-based is very high. Also, the number of organizations that use PHP-based tools is also high. The following image shows the popularity of the programming languages (Source: `http://www.tiobe.com/index.php/content/paperinfo/tpci/index.html`):

Position Feb 2009	Position Feb 2008	Delta in Position	Programming Language	Ratings Feb 2009	Delta Feb 2008	Status
1	1	=	Java	19.401%	-2.08%	A
2	2	=	C	15.837%	+0.98%	A
3	5	↑↑	C++	9.633%	+0.36%	A
4	3	↓	(Visual) Basic	8.843%	-2.76%	A
5	4	↓	PHP	8.779%	-1.11%	A
6	8	↑↑	C#	5.062%	+0.55%	A
7	7	=	Python	4.567%	-0.20%	A
8	6	↓↓	Perl	4.117%	-2.09%	A
9	9	=	Delphi	3.624%	+0.83%	A
10	10	=	JavaScript	3.540%	+1.21%	A
11	11	=	Ruby	3.278%	+1.42%	A
12	12	=	D	1.259%	+0.07%	A
13	13	=	PL/SQL	0.988%	+0.01%	A
14	14	=	SAS	0.835%	-0.11%	A
15	22	↑↑↑↑↑↑↑	Logo	0.813%	+0.50%	A--
16	17	↑	Pascal	0.689%	+0.24%	B
17	29	↑↑↑↑↑↑↑↑↑↑	ABAP	0.574%	+0.42%	B
18	21	↑↑↑	ActionScript	0.539%	+0.22%	B
19	26	↑↑↑↑↑↑↑	RPG (AS/400)	0.505%	+0.33%	B
20	18	↓↓	Lua	0.487%	+0.10%	B

The leading programming languages, Java, C, and C++, are very different form PHP. Java and C++ are used to implement enterprise as well as desktop applications. Many people still use C to implement systems software such as operating systems. Even the PHP engine is implemented in C. On the other hand, PHP is popular in a very different domain, namely **Web Programming**. As you can see, PHP is the leader when it comes to web-based programming.

Be it that your software project is using PHP or a tool based on PHP, given the complexity of today's software, you need a team of people. In other words, the days when one person could handle the development of a platform are long gone. Today's web applications are much more complex compared to the private home pages. For example, the PHP-based web application platforms like Flickr are quite complex web applications that are completely written in PHP. We are also seeing that blogging web applications are replacing private web sites at a very fast rate, and the blogging platforms are completely implemented in PHP.

In this chapter, you will learn:

- The need for teams for PHP projects
- How software engineering principles help with PHP projects
- The need for a process for PHP projects
- Dividing the project problem and conquering it
- How patterns help with PHP projects
- Using tools to manage the development and collaboration within the PHP team

Need for teams

We need the help of a team of people to successfully implement a solution to a complex problem. When we are trying to implement a solution for some problem, one of the obvious questions would be whether to implement the solution on our own or to look for ready made solutions which are available out there. There are many hosted solutions that can be found on the Internet for individual use these days. For example, you could go to a web hosting site and deploy your web site based on WordPress. You can also use one of many blogging tools and make it your home page. So if the task is simple, there is no point having a team of PHP developers to do the job. If the problem that we are looking to solve is complex, and if there are no readymade solutions available out there, we need to form a team to help solve the problem. Sometimes, we'll be able to find open source projects that solve the problem that we have been looking to solve. However, most of the open source projects are looking to solve generic problems. Most of the enterprises would have unique business problems to be solved. Hence, we might need a team of developers to implement that custom solution for the enterprise.

Implementing a more customized, value added, enterprise applications requires a team of developers. This is required, especially, given today's competitive marketplace, and given that almost all organizations make use of information technology. It is not the mere existence of a software application that matters most today. Rather, the application should meet the expectations of the enterprise, by being agile, flexible, and designed to deal with the ever changing business environment. For example, take a developer portal; you can easily use a content management system such as Drupal or Joomla! for hosting it. However, to customize it to meet the organizational objectives and maintain it over time, you might need more than one PHP developer—and that is a team.

If you look into a more complex enterprise scenario, such as online trading or social networking, your team could consist of around 10 to 100 people, or even more. Many PHP-based dynamic web sites could be managed effectively with about two good PHP developers. However, the number of members that you need in a team is very much dependant on the nature of the PHP project at hand. Apart from the design and coding activities, we need to take into account the testing and documentation effort in a project. We might also need to take into account the effort required to maintain the software, providing bug fixes, and facilitating change requests.

So it is obvious that you need a team, and you might already be part of a team. Perhaps this is the reason why you are reading this book, or you might want to join on organization where there are teams.

Software engineering principles to help

People have worked as teams on software projects for many years. Can the same techniques be used for your team PHP project? Yes they can. Then why read this book, and not read a regular book on software engineering? It is always good to have an understanding of software engineering principles, but in this book, we will explore how to blend the simplicity and power of PHP with evolving software engineering principles and tools. For example, how do you blend the agile process with tools such as Wikis and forums? This book will guide you to improve your success rate with projects, involving PHP.

In software engineering, there is a concept called **process rigor**. Based on the nature of the team and the technologies used, you can afford to vary the rigor with which you follow the process. You need not stick to the theory of the process, rather follow it the way that is most suited for your team. The process should help you get there and build a quality product. The process should help, and not hinder.

Many people associate PHP with simplicity and overlook the need to be declined when working with a team. This is also partly related to the fact that many complex programming constructs can be implemented very simply with PHP. For example, compare Java code for reading a file with that of PHP.

The following is the Java code for reading a file:

```java
import java.io.*;

class ReadFile {

public static void main(String args[])
{
  try
  {
    BufferedReader in = new BufferedReader(
    new FileReader("test.txt"));
    String str;
    while ((str = in.readLine()) != null)
    {
      System.out.println(str);
    }
  }
  catch (IOException e)
  {
  }
  finally
  {
    in.close();
  }
}
```

The following is the PHP code for reading a file:

```php
<?php
echo file_get_contents("test.txt");
?>
```

However, the fact that the programming language is simple and powerful does not mean that the nature of the software that you develop is simple. PHP is simple because it is less strict compared to Java or C++. Typepage, syntax alternatives, flexible parameter width, and so on, make it easier for writing something in a quick 'n' dirty style. Unfortunately, that is one of the areas where it gets complex for big projects with teams. If you give more parameters than the function reads, nothing will notify you. If you take the size of the API as criterion of simplicity, Java should be simpler than PHP because there are some functions, like `System.arraycopy()`, `String.endsWith()`, that you would need to implement by hand in PHP. So while PHP has evolved to a level where it can be used for complex projects, we also need to pay attention to these finer aspects that decide our success.

When you learn the programming language, you often worked on your own, but on your day job you need to work with other people. What you develop needs to work with what others develop. And if you build **Application Programming Interfaces (APIs)**, others need to use those and you also need to use APIs implemented by others. APIs are the means by which we can share the functionality that we implement with other developers. When a certain PHP class or function has widespread use, we can hide the implementation details behind the API and share only the API with the rest of the world. This is a very powerful mechanism while breaking down the system into manageable sub-parts and getting various team members to work on them.

Use a process

Therefore, you need some discipline, and a process. You need to learn how to work in parallel with others on different aspects of the same project. The parts from different developers will be integrated together at some point in time, and once integrated, they need to work seamlessly. Having said that, the PHP project team — that works on the PHP project for an organization — can also benefit from the luxury of the PHP language, being powerful and flexible. Therefore, you do not need a rigorous process either.

So where is the fine balance? Many software professionals now turn to agile processes. PHP teams can greatly benefit from an agile process, because PHP can help you live with agile values.

The agile process focuses on the agility of the team and the team working on the project focuses more on the delivery of a quality project, rather than getting stuck in a rigorous process. Rather than focusing on following the process, the agile principles focus on getting things done and getting them delivered to the client.

The values emphasized by agile methodology are:

Individuals and interactions over processes and tools

Working software over comprehensive documentation

Customer collaboration over contract negotiation

Responding to change over following a plan

(Source: www.agilemanifesto.org)

It is evident from the previously stated agile values that we are more focused on making customers happy by trying to deliver what the customers want.

Divide and conquer

Two minds are better than one. The whole is greater than the sum. You need a team because the problem at hand is difficult. However, you need to be organized and have discipline in the team in order to be successful. The best way to attack a complex problem is to break it down, into separate manageable parts.

When the problem is broken down, each sub problem could be solved in order to solve the whole problem. In the break down phase, it is a good practice to adhere to separation of concerns principle. For example, the user interface deals with presenting the application to the user. Based on inputs provided with the user interface, you carry out the business logic processing. For example, let's say that there is an application to help users query for the values of different stocks. The presentation would let the user enter a stock symbol. Once the user submits the form, the stock symbol would be sent to the backend, and the business logic would try and locate the quote for the given symbol. There isn't much business processing in here, just a query. However, in the next step of the application, the user might want to buy some stocks. At the presentation layer, the user will specify the symbol, and the quantity that he or she wishes to buy. When this request is submitted, the business logic layer would extract the stock price for the given symbol from the data layer, multiply that by the number of stocks that the user wants to buy, and provide that to the presentation layer. The presentation layer would display the total value to the user.

Here, presentation and business logics are separate concerns. The Business Logic Layer can also be broken into computations and retrieving and storing to persisted data storage. Computation is a separate concern compared to data storage. As an example, retrieving the price for a given stock symbol from the database is one aspect and computing the total cost using the price and the number of stocks is another.

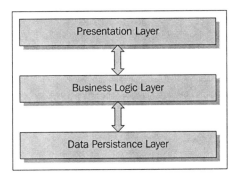

Once the problem is broken down based on separate concerns, you can get different members of the team to work on different aspects of the application.

In a single PHP script, all aspects, such as presentation, computation, and data retrieval, could be done very easily. You can present a form to the user, get input, connect to the DB, retrieve relevant data based in input values, do the computation, and send the result back. However, that is something a novice programmer would do. An experienced programmer would use the **MVC (Model View Controller)** pattern. Patterns are proven solutions to well known problems. The rationale is that, the kind of problems that we are trying to solve when implementing a system, must have been seen by other developers in the history of computing, and they must also have solved those. Therefore, rather than trying to reinvent the wheel, we can benefit from the kind of solutions that has been used.

If the system is complex, using patterns alone would not help. This is because there are a few aspects that you need to address.

Guarantee reuse

Make sure that common functionality and common classes are not duplicated and not written multiple times by various team members.

In the evolution of programming techniques, people have moved from functional programming to **Object-Oriented Programming (OOP)**. In the functional approach, a program is a collection of function calls. While this technique helped us achieve some level of reuse, when it comes to maintaining the system, the life gets harder. This is because the data manipulation in the system is spread across the system, and controlling which function changes which set of data is hard.

To solve the problem of uncontrolled data, people came up with the concept of encapsulation is the object-oriented paradigm. The rationale was to encapsulate the data and functions that process those together into a concept called an object class. Related data would be kept together, along with the methods that process them, so that it is clear, which method changes which data. In object-oriented programming, a program is a collection of objects, and an object is an instance of a class, which encapsulates the data and related functions.

While in functional programming, the units being reused are functions, in object-oriented programming, the unit of reuse is a class. The key difference is that in a functional case, there is no control over the data reuse, while in object-oriented programming, the object classes being reused have both data and methods that process those encapsulated together.

Be it fictional programming that you are using or object-oriented programming, you need to make a conscious effort to pay attention to reuse. It must also be noted that the object-oriented programming style encourage reuse naturally, and therefore it is easier to achieve reuse with object oriented design, compared to a functional design.

Guarantee integration

The 'I did my part my way' kind of mindset is not going to work in a team setup. Especially when it comes to API design, we must find common ground, and make sure that all of the members of the team understand the conventions and norms used. Even when doing the internal implementation, the individual programmer can tend to assume that it is his or her own code and follow personal preferences. But in a complex system, when you think of bug fixing or improving the functionality of a given piece of code and the original programmer is not around, the other team members should be able to manage the situation. Therefore, even the variable naming and the algorithms used have significance in a project done by a team of developers.

Make sure that what you do does not break what others have done and vice versa. After all, everything that the members of the team implement needs to work together as one system.

Changes are inevitable. Any living software system must change and evolve, to adapt to the changing real-world conditions, for that system to be useful.

Prevent regression

When multiple people work in parallel, the chances of bugs being introduced in the system is very high. It is always a good practice to keep the system at a working and operational state, irrespective of missing and yet to be implemented features. One of the most well known techniques to keep the system working all of the time is to make sure that there is a comprehensive set of unit tests. At least all of the major functionality, if not all functionality, must be covered with a unit test. This way, whenever you make a change or update, we can run the test suite to ensure that nothing has broken. That simply ensures that the team would end up with a high quality working system. Deferring bugs until late is not a good practice, and will demand more cycles from the team members in the long run.

Vertical versus horizontal division

Earlier, we discussed the divide and conquer approach for a complex solution, and stressed the need for separation of concerns. When separating concerns, you can either divide it horizontally or vertically. An example of dividing horizontally would be to address the presentation layer by one team, business logic by another team, and database layer by yet another team.

Dividing vertically would mean to separate the system logically based on various functionality. For example, listing the products, purchasing a selected product, and product delivery related tasks could be handled by different sub-teams. The sub-team would handle all of the functionalities in the completion; meaning presentation, business logic, as well as data persistence, for each functionality would be entirely handled by the respective sub-team.

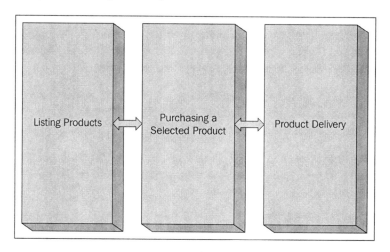

Whatever the separation style, the cross-cutting concerns come into play. Cross-cutting concerns are those aspects of the system that has system wide impact. One important example is logging. We need to use a consistent approach, especially in the format of log messages, throughout the system. Another important example is authentication. We have to be consistent with respect to authentication throughout the system. We are not supposed to use different authentication mechanisms for the same system. If we do, there are chances that we might leave behind some security holes in the systems. We might have to verify all different authentication mechanisms into the system. If we leave behind even one authentication mechanism by mistake, that would open up a possible back door into the system — risking the security of the entire system. Therefore, authentication needs to be handled in a consistent manner throughout the system. Therefore, we are better off providing a single, unified authentication library for the entire system. And one sub-team should work on that aspect. This would not only ensure consistency, but would also ensure enhanced reuse. Reuse will be enhanced because one interface would be used by all other modules in the system for authentication. In addition, this approach of addressing cross-cutting concerns by a given sub-team eases integration pains. If each sub-system used its own security module for authentication, then when all of those sub-parts are put together, in other words integrated, there would be numerous integration pains.

For example, if one module did not take all aspects into account while authenticating a user, that might open up a security hole in the overall system. If there was one module to address security, you can fix it and the improvement would be reflected across the entire system. Fixing each module would be really painful. The approach where cross-cutting concerns such as security are separated prevents regression issues. If the security module is broken, it is obvious where to fix it.

Consistency also applies to the presentation layer. Often, we use a common template to guarantee a consistent look and feel. A template helps us to define the common subset of the web pages in our presentation layer. When the data gets updated, we just need to fill in the placeholders with those data into the template. This way, we do not have to worry about the entire page all of the time. In addition, we need to have consistency across all web pages in a unified system. We can use a common template to achieve this, and when we want to update the look and feel of the entire web site, we just need to change the template and the entire site would get updated. This way, we can save time and energy spent on changing hundreds of pages. It is a common practice for developers to use tools or a library to help with the template. This is due to the benefits such as consistent API, specific feature sets, and recognizable template markup across the project that the template engines provide us. This way, system maintenance and management becomes very easy. But that does not mean that we do not need to pay attention to consistency when developing content to be embedded into the templates.

Even the content that is to be embedded could have layout concerns. For example, where in the page the content will be placed and how the content will be presented. The content that fills in the main templates would come from modules, which again are in the form of smaller templates. But when we choose the layout and the formation of the content within those, we need to ensure consistency. For example, if the data is presented as a list of bullets, would that fit into the rest of the larger template layout? Should that content be a set of links? After all, the entire page that the user sees is a single web page formed using multiple sub parts.

Therefore, in practice, it is easier to have the entire system broken in terms of horizontal concerns, to achieve team success. It makes it easy to deal with changes. On one hand, there are people who know the domain, and on the other hand, we can easily identify the areas to be changed and also easily pin point the problem location if we happen to run into bugs.

Bugs are inevitable, and a complex system will have bugs. The success criterion is how fast we can locate those bugs in order to fix them. In my experience, it is not bug fixing that takes time, but rather locating the bugs in terms of understanding where and why things are going wrong.

We can try and reduce the number of bugs through the process. However, changes in design and implementation would always lead to bugs.

Continuous integration

Continuous integration helps when it comes to easing integration pains. In the context of a PHP project, continuous integration means that, rather than trying to deploy only those scripts that one or few developers implement on a developer's machine, all useable libraries and PHP code developed so far, needs to be put together by all developers in their local machines and test their own bits and pieces. Alternatively, all of the team members can use a staging server onto which they deploy all of the PHP code that they develop, at least on a daily basis, and run the tests on that staging server. This ensures that all individual pieces are integrated together on a regular basis.

If separate sub-teams of the team keep on working on the independent aspects for too long, then the chances of surprises when the system is integrated is higher. It is a good practice to integrate on a daily basis. This will make the overall system break too often, but at the same time, you can solve the problems early. As mentioned earlier, a common staging server can be used by the team for daily testing. It is a bad idea to use the live site for this kind of testing. This model saves time over time. For example, the presentation layer, that is the web page, might have assumed an older interface on the back end. The business logic library implementers added another parameter to the method being invoked. For the front end, this might mean an additional element in the inputs form, and these kinds of changes are accumulated over time. For a project where development is very active, this may mean a drastic change—even within a week. The back-end folks might have made assumptions too, about the front end, when they implemented their code, so those need to be fixed earlier in the development cycle as well.

These sorts of drastic changes and lack of understanding would prevail in the early stages of a project. The developers in the team would be learning what is required by users and also how to design the system. Therefore, a prototyping model would help a great deal in here, where the team develops something for the sole purpose of understanding the system and get over the assumptions.

Obviously, continuous integration requires aggressive code sharing. Therefore, you must seek help from a code sharing system, for example, **Subversion (SVN)**. SVN is a source code revisioning system that can be used to keep track of the differences in the source code, but it also can act as a source code repository. So in addition to comparing differences between your local changes and the latest code in the central code repository, you can also make use of SVN to merge your changes to the central repository, so that you share your local changes with the others. This way, it becomes a source code sharing system.

You also need unit tests to verify and guard against regression. As it was mentioned earlier, unit testing helps us guard against regression issues. We need all developers working on the project to write their own unit tests that test each area that they develop in isolation. Once we have those unit tests, life becomes easy to test the system when upgrading and changing the system. Unit tests can be automated, so that the developers need not worry about running the test framework manually. To make sure that unit tests are really run, we can integrate those to the staging server update process. This ensures that whenever a developer adds something to the staging server, the entire unit testing framework is run. If anything is broken, a notification could be triggered.

All of this needs to be controlled carefully. Therefore, you need the application of software engineering principles. When we talk about integration, there are numerous practices that we can learn from the software engineering principles. Defining a process for change control, techniques to be followed when implementing testing, and quality assurance practices are some examples where established software engineering principles can help us.

Patterns as solutions

Patterns can help make the software more robust and capable of dealing with change.

For many PHP applications, MVC is the most useful pattern. This is because PHP is used for web-based applications. However, they are not just web pages, but are applications based on backend business logic. There are numerous other patterns such as observer/observable, iterator/for each, and handler chain, which can be of use in the design of the system.

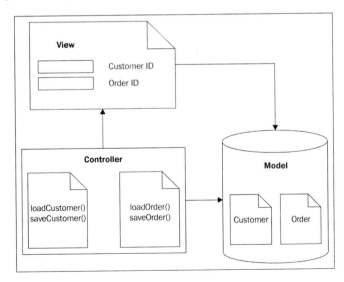

> **Model View Controller**
>
> **Model**: It represents the data on which the application operates
>
> **View:** It renders the data from the model into a form suitable for interaction, typically a user interface
>
> **Controller:** It responds to events, typically user interactions, and may invoke changes on the model

Applying a pattern just saves time and effort. We need to be aware of the problems and solutions that the patterns try to address in general, to make use of patterns effectively. A pattern is a description of a problem and the potential solution to it. There is no standard answer for all problems that we find when working on a software project. So it helps to be aware of the problems, and be capable of adapting the solution suggested by the pattern to suite the problem at hand. Many software professionals have used patterns over the years and the patterns are proven to work. You might have used patterns without knowing that it is a pattern, but not knowing the principles would lead to creative chaos. It is always advisable to spend some time and learn the principles behind the software patterns for any developer. Having the knowledge about problems that can appear, and the potential solutions to those problems, adds to the experience of a good PHP developer. The effort spent on understanding the patters would help the PHP team members in the long run. It would even be a good idea to train the entire team on patterns with hands-on examples in the early stages of a project.

Many frameworks or tools support patterns out of the box. All that is required is to apply the pattern carefully to your application. It is also important to make sure that everyone in the team understands the pattern, as well as how the pattern applies to the problem at hand.

Process for success

A process helps people to streamline what everyone is doing to make sure a successful product, in our case the software, is built. As mentioned earlier, given that PHP is simple, people tend to overlook the need for a process in PHP-based software projects. A process that defines the set of activities, the ordering of those activities, input and outputs of those activities, and is followed in a given sequence, produces the right outcomes. For example, we need to analyze the system, design it, implement it, test it, and deploy the system into production, followed by maintenance.

Complex software needs some process in place. It is not required to be too religious about the process. However, you need to pick and choose the right process for you and make sure that all members of the team on board follow the process as expected.

Today, many people follow an agile process, or agile-like processes. The focus of an agile process is to make sure that we effectively deal with change and deliver the product sooner. Earlier in the chapter, the agile principles were introduced.

The values of the process focus on getting things done sooner and in an easy to turn around manner.

 The agile process promotes development iterations where tasks are done in small increments with minimal planning, rather than long-term planning. Success with an agile process also depends on teamwork, collaboration, and process adaptability throughout the life cycle of the project.

Tools

For any project, we need the help of tools in order to be successful. Earlier in this chapter, it was explained how complex today's software projects are. We discussed the need for teams of software developers. Likewise, tools are essential for the success of software projects these days.

Tools make sure that we make fewer errors, be consistent with our approach to design, development testing, and that we are effective and productive in the way we approach the project.

We can seek the help of tools for source control, automated unit testing, issue tracking, communication and collaboration. Without proper tools, it would have been hard, if not impossible, to achieve success in these areas of a project.

Source code control

Source code revisions should be maintained so you can revert to an old code if necessary. Source code control is a must. It is especially helpful in situations where you are troubleshooting to locate the cause of an issue. If you know a broken feature was working some time back, you always can revert back to a known point and try to locate the change in code that caused the problems.

Source control also helps to keep in touch with what others are doing to the code by having a look at the change summaries. Most source code control systems support a means of evaluating the difference between the central source code repository and the local copy that a developer has, that he or she might have changed. With SVN, all that you need to do is to run the following command:

```
svn diff
```

When you work in a team, collective code ownership is a must. The commands such as svn diff make your life easy when living in a world where the source code is shared.

There are various source code controlling tools around. For example, SVN (http://subversion.tigris.org/) and GIT (http://git-scm.com/) are the most popular source code controlling tools nowadays. We will visit source control tools, and more importantly best practices, later in this book.

The concept of revisions, as shown in the preceding screenshot, helps to keep track of the changes that each developer in the team has done on the PHP source code. Whenever a change is done and is integrated with the central source code repository, it will be identified by a unique revision number. Revision numbers given to changes are continuous, and that helps to figure out the exact sequence of changes that has gone into the source code between two points in time. This makes it much easier to pinpoint problem causing changes, from among a sequence of changes that has taken place on the source code.

Continuous builds

Make sure that everyone builds the system regularly, at least once a day. If the system is too large, make nightly builds. A build is a package where everyone's changes to the source code are included, and all of the elements of the software system are present. When the developers are busy with their own sub-modules, PHP classes, interfaces and unit testing the sub-modules, it can be easily overlooked to put all pieces of the system together and give it a test run.

For PHP, there is no compilation involved. There are cases where packages can be compiled and packaged in PHP, which correlates to something similar to building. For example, when developing PEAR packages and creating automated documentation, you would build the system. So what does it really mean to say 'do continuous builds?' Why bother with builds at all when working with PHP? There are numerous use cases in which continuous builds come into play. For example, those who are working on the database might change the database configuration or data schema. People who are working on libraries might refactor their code and change script paths or method signatures. This is possible, because everyone is busy developing in parallel. For maximum utilization of team resources, especially people, as well as to deliver the system sooner, you need to work in parallel. There is a drastic difference between working in parallel and deploying in parallel. When delivering a system, we need to define a set of milestones that we want to achieve as the project progresses. Each milestone would be achieved with a series of work iterations. Before deploying to the live system, for the purpose of integration testing, we would need to deploy the milestones to a staging server. Continuous builds are meant for testing with staging deployments and not for the real-life deployment of an application.

Due to the dynamic nature of the project and the way the team members' work, when you put all of the pieces together, the final picture would look drastically different from what you would see in isolation. You need to make sure that everyone sees the big picture on a regular basis.

When you are working with a team of people, there are various sub-groups within the team, who are experts in various domains. Some are designers and developers. Some are user interface design experts. Some are experts in testing and quality assurance. When you are working in a project, you need to keep all of these team members posted about the latest status. The designers, developers, and UI designers need to know what progress has been made so far. You also need to give the latest picture to the **quality assurance (QA)** team on a regular basis. In traditional software engineering, the quality assurance team would wait until they are given a release pack or a QA build. But with agile process, you can make the QA team be part of the daily process, helping to find issues on a daily basis. Continuous integration eliminates big surprises in terms of integration efforts.

Issue tracking

Talking about QA, keeping track of issues in the system is very important. It makes life easier when you know what issues were found, what issues are still open, what were fixed, and when those were fixed. Sometimes, due to regression, some issues might even get reopened.

You can assign issues to team members and schedule issues so that other stakeholders of the project get to know when the issues will be attended to.

Not only bugs, but also improvements, wish lists, tasks, and so on can be tracked with an issue tracking system. This makes sure that all good ideas are noted and attended to at some point in time.

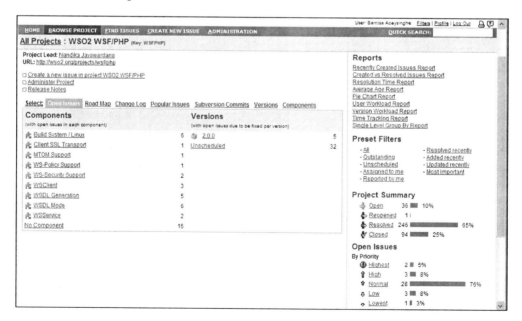

There are numerous tools that are available, both open source and commercial for bug tracking. Jira (`http://www.atlassian.com/software/jira/`) and Bugzilla (`http://www.bugzilla.org/`) are two popular bug tracking tools.

Communication

Communication is a critical factor for the success of a software project team. No matter how technically competent your team members are, if the communication is not perfect, the entire team could fail.

If the interface between presentation and business logic layers are to be changed, then all of the members of both the presentation and business logic sub-teams should know about the change. It is not only the fact that the interface is going to change that needs to be communicated, but also the rationale for the change, who gets affected, what to expect, and what needs to be done by each member to make the change successful.

There are many forms of communication, and there are many tools to help you with communication. You can have face to face meetings and design and code review sessions. Wikis for documenting and noting down discussion points, are shown in the following screenshot:

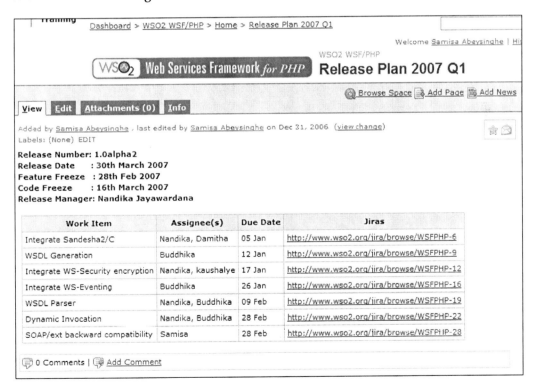

Mailing lists and forums can be used for discussions. Likewise, chat rooms can be used for discussions. However, discussing in a chat room is very different from discussing in a forum or mailing list. A chat room is real time (synchronous), whereas a mailing list or a forum has a time lag involved (asynchronous). Unlike in a chat room, you need to wait until the others respond to the emails or the forum entry. On the other hand, mailing lists and forums are archived (as shown in the following screenshot), so they can be used as informal documentation as well. Instant messaging is another great channel that can be used for communication. Instant messaging also comes with great archiving facilities.

Various forms of communication can be used for various communication needs of the team. It is helpful to ensure that every team member understands the need for communication as well as the means of communication to use, based on the information being communicated.

We will discuss the tools and techniques for communication, in detail, later in the book.

Summary

In this chapter, we discussed why we need teams to work on software projects, and in particular, on PHP software projects. Along with the evolving real world requirements, the PHP software too needs to evolve, thus they become complex over time.

Since PHP is being used for complex enterprise systems nowadays, we need help from the software engineering principles to deal with the PHP projects. However, given the power and simplicity of PHP, we can choose the rigour process to suite our needs.

Separation of concerns helps us deal with complex projects, dividing the problem into smaller, more manageable parts. Dividing the system based on cross-cutting concerns help teams to deal with complexities easier.

Continuous integration, use of patterns and using the right process, help achieve team success with any software project. For PHP, MVC is the most used pattern. Given the power and simplicity of the PHP programming language, we can leverage the agile process values for PHP projects.

Source control tools, issue tracking tools, continuous builds, and tools that help with proper team communication such as Wikis, forums, mailing lists, and instant messaging chat rooms can be used to improve your team PHP project success.

In the next chapter, we will explore the MVC pattern in more detail and discuss how we can ensure a team can get involved with the MVC pattern in a PHP software project.

2

MVC and Software Teams

The software patterns help software professionals to reuse the proven solutions to well-known problems. **MVC (Model-View-Controller)** is one such design pattern, mostly used in applications where user interfaces are involved.

Many PHP applications will have a web-based user interface. Even if you develop a PHP utility library to be used by other programmers, when they use that library in the real world, there will be some presentation logic, in other words a user interface, involved.

In this chapter, we will learn:

- The software design patterns
- The MVC pattern
- How MVC can help in a PHP project
- Implementing MVC with a team
- Integration challenges

Software design patterns

The rationale for the use of patterns is very simple. We face problems when we develop software. We might face problems on making decisions about which algorithms to use, what is the most suitable design, what techniques to use, and what modules to use. The chances that the same kind of problem has been encountered by some other software professionals are very high. If someone else has faced the same problem before us, the chances of them having solved the problem is very high. If someone already solved the kind of problem that we are trying to solve, we are better off learning from that solution which is already available, rather than trying to reinvent the wheel.

Every problem is unique. Therefore, every solution should also be unique. So how can we use someone else's solution to our problem? The rationale for the use of software patterns is not about picking up ready made solutions to problems. Rather, the patterns guide us on how to approach a problem. In the previous chapter, we discussed dividing and conquering a problem. When we divide a larger problem into smaller manageable pieces, those smaller problems can seem familiar. For example, we might need to sort a list of elements, before displaying them. We can use a sorting algorithm here, and there are plenty of implementations of sorting algorithms out there.

The sorting algorithm is more of a ready made solution. When it comes to design, the patterns can guide us in the right direction in terms of what is to be done. For example, the MVC pattern helps us to figure out how to separate out presentation from business logic and data. That is just a guideline. We can use the guidelines and implement our solution based on that. Software patterns help us reuse known solutions to common problems, and then customize those to our needs.

 A **design pattern** is a general reusable solution to a commonly occurring problem in software design.

When software design patterns are documented, there are some elements that must be present in the documentation to help understand the pattern better. Some of the most important documentation elements for a design pattern are:

- **Name**: A unique name that helps identify the pattern and can be used when referring to the pattern
- **Intent**: The reasons and goals for using the pattern
- **Motivation**: The problem scenario and the context in which this pattern can be used
- **Solution**: The solution this pattern provides to the problem at hand

The use of design patterns helps us solve our problems in a more effective manner, saving time and making sure of quality solutions. There are multiple benefits in the use of design patterns:

- Learning from others' experiences, especially from experts in the software field
- Using the guaranteed solution to a problem at hand, because the problem has been already solved and is proven to work
- Saving time by not re-inventing a solution that has already been found
- Helping eliminate software design issues, and cut down troubleshooting and debugging time
- Using common jargon to describe problems and solutions can help a great deal with communication, which is critical for team success by allowing everyone to share knowledge with ease

MVC pattern

MVC is a widely known pattern that guides us to separate the presentation, logic, and data in an application where there is a user interface involved.

Intent

In many software applications, we need to retrieve data from a data store and display it for the user. If the user changes the data, the software application needs to store the updates in the data store. Because the flow of information is between the data store and the user interface, we are inclined to tie the data storage and the user interface together. This will reduce the amount of coding and also improve the application performance. However, this approach has some significant problems. The user interface tends to change much more frequently than the data storage system. Therefore, we should be able to change the user interface, without having to worry about the data storage.

For example, let's say that the data access logic and the presentation logic are in the same PHP script. We connect to the database, retrieve the data, and display that in a table. You first have the table headers declared, then the database access logic, and finally you use the results from the query and print them in a loop inside data table elements. The presentation logic, which displays the data in a table and the data access logic, which accesses the data elements from the result set, are in the same PHP code. Now imagine that we need to change the presentation from a table to an ordered list. As the presentation and data access are in the same PHP file, we need to take great care that we do not change the data access logic while changing the presentation logic.

Having code that ties those two layers together would affect the data store, even though we just want to change the user interface. Another problem with coupling the data and user interface pieces together is that business applications tend to incorporate business logic that will be more complex than just transmitting data from user interface and the data store. We might also want to isolate business logic processing to help us deal with software application complexities better.

Motivation

How do we modularize the user interface functionality of a web application so that you can easily modify the individual parts, such as the user interface, business logic, and data storage?

Solution

The following diagram shows the high-level formation of the three elements in MVC — the model, view, and the controller:

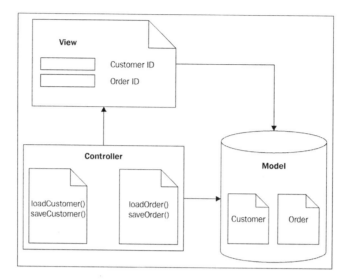

Model

The model represents the data on which the application operates. The model manages the behavior and data of the application domain. It responds to requests for information from the view and responds to instructions to change information from the controller. In the context of PHP, the model corresponds to the database schema. The database management system plays a key role in PHP applications when it comes to data persistence.

View

The view renders the data from the model into a form suitable for interaction, typically a user interface. In other words, the view manages the display of information. In the context of PHP applications, the view corresponds to the HTML-based presentation that is delivered to the user, to be displayed with a web browser.

Controller

The controller responds to events, typically user interactions, and may invoke changes on the model or the view. In the context of PHP applications, the controller is the actual PHP code that deals with the business processing. It also couples with the HTTP logic — given that the PHP application's main delivery channel to the users is HTTP.

Both the view and the controller depend on the model. However, the model does not depend on the view or the controller. This is one of the key benefits of the separation of concerns. This separation allows the model to be implemented and tested independent of the visual presentation. In web applications, the separation between view and controller is very well-defined. For example, the browser which presents the view to the user is completely separate from the server side components handling the HTTP request. So even though the interface rendered on the browser is generated on the server side, the interface that is meant to be rendered on the browser (the HTML page prepared to be sent to the browser), is completely separate form the logical elements that process and compute the data to be presented to the user. The MVC pattern is a fundamental design pattern for the separation of user interface logic from business logic.

How MVC can help

MVC is a very good example of separation of concerns. It helps us to break down a system into view (presentation layer), controller (business logic layer), and model (data layer). Let us look at a simple example.

Assume that we want to store data about people in our system. We want to store the name and age of these people. Rather than the age, we will store the date of birth — this makes the application more agile over the years. As people grow older, we will not need to change the database content. Suppose we want to list all of the teens in the system. For this, we query the database for the date of birth, compute the age of the person at business logic layer, and present the view to the user. If the user wants to sort every one by age to locate the youngest ones, the user should be able to do that on the view — click on the title of the age column, and the sorting will be done.

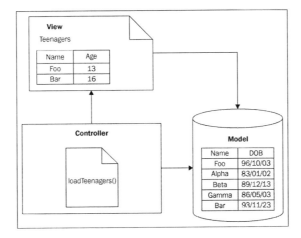

The preceding image shows the mapping of MVC into a real implementation. The model stores names and dates of birth for the people. The controller loads the teenagers form the model, based on the simple logic implemented in the `loadTeenagers()` function. The data set provided by the controller is then presented to the user. When the user is looking at the view, he might want to sort the list either by the name or by the age. So the user will click on the column header. Based on the column clicked, the presentation layer, that is the browser would be able to come up with the correct sorting using some AJAX magic.

MVC helps with change

Dealing with change is one of the key challenges in any software system. Therefore, PHP-based systems also need to face that reality. Changes can be of many forms and can happen at any layer of the software system.

Let's look at a library system as an example.

Say that the library used to rent only books, but now it plans to add DVDs. The data model must change, because the information to be stored for a book is not the same as for a DVD. For example, there is no ISBN for a DVD. This change might not affect the business logic (controller) or presentation layer (view), for renting aspect, if the item borrowing policies for both the item types (that is, books and DVDs) are the same. For example, the borrowing policy is two books for two weeks or two DVDs for two weeks or one book and one DVD for two weeks. However, note that the data input forms must be updated, and we will need to add new forms for DVDs. There are two different presentation forms for registering books and DVDs into the system:

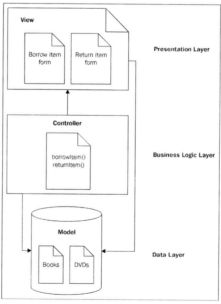

After some time, the librarian or the management committee of the library may decide to change the renting policy, rather than keeping the same policy for different items such as books and DVDS. Earlier, two books, two DVDs, or a book and a DVD could be borrowed for 2 weeks. Considering the increased demand, now the policy is to be changed for DVDs. Only one DVD can be borrowed by a single user and only for one week. This affects the business logic layer (the controller) and if the system is designed in synchronization with MVC, neither the presentation layer nor the DB layer need to be changed.

Earlier, the logic was:

```
if ($numberOfItemsBorrowed < 2)
   borrowItem ($itemNo)
```

But now the logic changes to:

```
if ($item is book AND $numberOfBooksBorrowed < 2)
   borrowItem($itemNo)
else if ($item is DVD AND $numberOfDVDsBorrowed < 1)
   borrowItem ($itemNo)
```

After some time, there could be another change request. Earlier, the same form was used to borrow books and DVDs, and the librarian at the counter did not see the current borrowing information on screen. The librarian just entered the item information into the form, and would get to know if the user was really able to borrow a book or a DVD only after submitting the form. If the borrowing was successful, the user will get a success message and if there was an error, an error message would have been displayed.

To improve ease of use, the librarian is requesting to see the current borrowings of a user, as a report, so that he can have a glance at the library user's item borrowing status.

This change is a user interface enhancement and only affects the presentation layer. We do not need to edit the business logic layer or the database layer for this enhancement. There is no workflow change associated here as the change is only to facilitate the need to information by the librarian.

As we can see, the MVC pattern helps a great deal when it comes to changing, enhancing, and evolving the system over time.

The MVC patterns help us to easily identify the areas of change and facilitate the change requests from system users. This is very useful in any software system, irrespective of the scale of the system.

In addition to helping us locate the piece of logic to be changed, an indirect advantage of MVC is that by isolating changes to a particular layer, it prevents regression issues in the system. One of the key challenges in changing a working system is the difficulty of making the change without breaking the existing functionality. If not for MVC, we might have a situation where we have mixed up the business logic, presentation, and data access. Therefore, a change done, say to improve presentation, cannot be guaranteed to not have affected the other areas.

In most of the systems, it is the business logic (in other words, controller) and the presentation layer (also known as view) that are likely to change more than the data model. In comparison to business logic, presentation is far more likely to change on a regular basis.

Business logic will need to change with the dynamic business environment. For example, the following situations would enforce changes to the business logic layer:

- Change in government regulations
- Business strategy changes by competitors
- Various market conditions

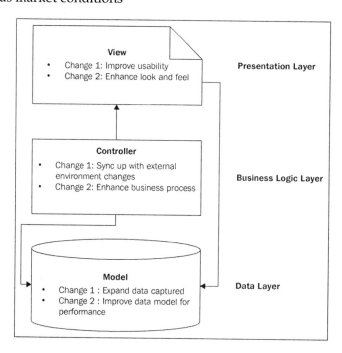

In most PHP applications, we might need to keep on improving the presentation to:

- Improve usability
- Enhance the look and feel

For example, we might decide to give a face lift by changing the entire look and feel, and thus aesthetics of the system. We shouldn't do this too often though, as the faithful users would be annoyed. In the current Internet space, **Search Engine Optimization (SEO)** is also a huge challenge. We should be able to change the titles and links of the pages, to facilitate SEO aspirations—especially in order to have meaningful and content dependant titles. Therefore, changes to the presentation layer might be regular—on a weekly basis, if not on a daily basis—to make it better as well as to achieve better rating with search engines (such as Google).

View can have dynamic components too, so that dynamic aspects like keyword integration are not hard-wired within a view, but can relate to controller variable assignment as well. This will make sure that we do not need to change the application every time the search engine keywords are changed.

Implementing MVC with a team

In the previous chapter, we discussed how separation of concerns would help when working with a team. We can divide the system into separate parts with independent concerns and get sub-teams to work on each separate aspect in parallel, and integrate all those individual pieces of the puzzle at a later stage.

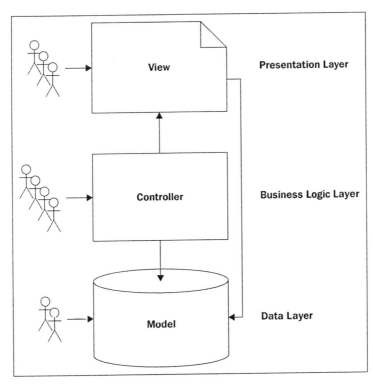

The preceding image shows how we can distribute our team to map the elements of MVC. Team members can be assigned to each layer, based on each person's expertise.

The MVC pattern helps us identify key layers of a system with ease. At the highest layer, we can divide the system into MVC and get the sub-teams to work on each aspect.

The simplest assignment is to assign each layer to a sub-team. Thus, presentation, business logic, and database layers will each be handled by a separate sub-team. You can have UI experts assigned to the presentation layer, database experts to the data layer, and those who have a good understanding with algorithms and who have a good knowledge of how the business works to the business layer.

Aspects of the presentation layer (view)

In a complex system of the system, even the sub-team might need to be further divided into various aspects of each layer. For example, the presentation layer, that is the view, would have various aspects to deal with, such as:

- Reports
- Output filtering
- Forms
- Input validation
- AJAX and DHTML
- Interfacing with control and model
- Presentation templates
- Graphics and styling
- UI testing

Based on the complexity, one or more individuals can own each space. If the system is small or medium scale, you could have one individual owning multiple aspects.

Complexity versus number of team members: While deciding on the number of people you'll need in a software team, it is important to understand the system complexity. System complexity is an indicator of the amount of work involved.

A simple criterion that can be used to gauge the complexity of the presentation layer is the total number of forms and reports that the system will have. It usually is the case that each and every form, and each and every report will have its own PHP file. So the presentation layer complexity measuring criteria can be defined in terms of the number of PHP scripts in the presentation layer.

One of the obvious concerns that can arise here is determining how we will know the number of PHP scripts that are going to be in the presentation layer during this planning phase of the project? This is because we have not done any coding as of now, and we are trying to gauge the complexity of the system. The idea here is to come up with some estimate of the number of forms and reports that will be there in the system. When we are gathering the user requirement, and analyzing the system, we can easily collect this data.

If available, we can make use of historical data on similar projects that we have done in the past. We can get the number of PHP files in the presentation layer, and correlate that to the current project we are going to work on.

When PHP logic is decoupled from the presentation specific aspects such as HTML, AJAX, XML, and so on, we need to take those into account as well, in order to gauge the complexity of the presentation layer.

 In general, number scripts in the overall system can be used to gauge the overall system complexity as well.

The diagram above shows an example form that the users can use to query for issues in a bug tracking system. This was taken form a hosted instance of a JIRA system for WSO2 WSF/PHP. As you can see, the form is quite complex, and can have serious backend controller logic associated with it. However, this form is a form with average complexity, and it is the number of these kinds of forms that you need to take into account when gauging system complexity.

Presentation layer complexity: The total number of forms and reports, in other words the total number of PHP scripts, in the presentation layer can be an indicator of presentation layer complexity.

The amount of aspects an individual can handle is based on the individual skills. Some individuals can handle multiple tasks whereas some would prefer to have focused work. Therefore, the task assignments need to be based on individual traits and preference.

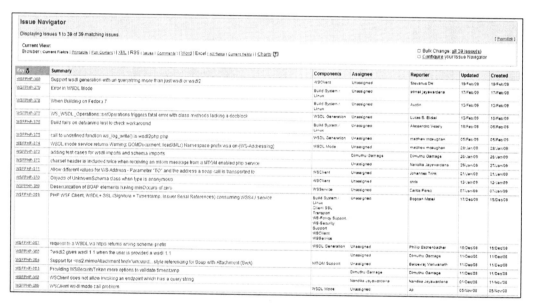

This is an example report, again from the JIRA issue tracking system of WSO2 WSF/PHP project. This is a report with average level of complexity. Note that the most important aspect of a report is the provision for the users to customize the report to their needs. The amount of customizability increased the complexity of the controller logic as well as the presentation layer logic.

The business logic layer, or the controller, in general would have the following areas to focus on:

- Data validation
- Providing interface to the presentation layer
- Using the database layer interface
- Algorithms
- Business domain specific processing

The controller takes care of the updates and access to the data. Therefore, at this layer, knowledge about the domain is critical.

The team members working at this layer should have the ability to learn domain specific knowledge. This is because when you move from one project to another, you need to learn new domains. It does not necessarily mean that the team members working at other layers do not need to know the domain. Rather, it is those who work on the business logic layer that need to have the greatest problem domain specific knowledge. Specifically, they need to learn the dynamics of the business.

Like in the case of the presentation layer, you can gauge the complexity of the business logic layer to determine how many team members to have in the sub-team and how to allocate work. For the business logic layer, the number of PHP classes in use, if it is an object-oriented system, or the number of functions in use, if it is a functional system, can provide us with a general idea on the complexity of the system.

Business Layer Complexity: The number of PHP classes, or the number of PHP functions in the business logic layer, can be an indicator of business logic layer complexity.

Model, or the data layer, also has different aspects to be taken into consideration:

- Database design
- Queries and stored procedures
- Object classes map to data objects
- Data access layer
- Interface to the business logic and presentation layers

Again, like in the business logic layer, the database design requires a considerable amount of domain knowledge. However, rather than the business dynamics, it is the entity relation model that you need to worry about at this layer. Entity relationship models are abstract representations of data and help us to capture the data model at a conceptual level.

When we are using PHP, we always have the luxury of the flexible database support that the PHP scripting language provides us. For example, we can make use of **PHP Data Objects (PDO)** — http://www.php.net/pdo — which abstracts out the data access layer. We can use this to the maximum, when dealing with model. The other aspect is the queries and stored procedures being used in this layer. All SQL is supposed to be written inside model, or the data access layer. These would be somewhat influenced by the business logic layer processing. Therefore, there should be good rapport between business logic layer folks and database layer folks. However, that should not lead to tight coupling of these layers. The stored procedures, if used, tend to be dependant on business logic. Therefore, it is advisable to refrain from using stored procedures as much as possible, as that can violate MVC principles.

The complexity of the database layer would be mainly governed by a couple of aspects. We can get a gauge of complexity looking at the number of tables in the database. However, this is very much a flat view, or in other words a static view, of the system. A more realistic view of system complexity would be indicated by the number of queries or prepared statements in use at the database layer. You can determine your team member assignments, based on these complexity measures at this layer.

 Data layer complexity: The number of database tables, or the number of queries and stored procedure in the data layer, can be an indicator of data layer complexity.

The overall team distribution

MVC provides us with a good frame work when separating concerns in a PHP-based project. At the highest level, we can break down the team into the three elements of this design pattern. Then, when we further drill down, we can further break down each layer, and assign independent tasks to each member of each sub-team. As always, the key challenge is to ensure that each piece of work, done by individuals at each layer, work with each other in a seamless manner. The advantage of using the MVC pattern is that, across layers, we have well defined integration points, at which we would worry about integration. So as long as all of M, V, and C, work on their own, it is only a matter of putting them together and they should work seamlessly.

Integration challenges

You will run in to integration challenges, first and foremost, if you did not adhere to the principles in the design pattern. The simplest thing to remember is not to cross boundaries and that is the basic idea of the separation of concerns.

Pay attention to **boundaries** in your design. Do not cross domains. The view should not control data or store data. Rather, it should only display data. Similarly, controller and model should focus on their respective responsibilities.

Always make sure that the team members of your team consciously ask the question, 'Is this within my boundary?'. The idea is to not pass the balls across to the others, but to stick to good design norms. The idea is pretty simple. The presentation should never process data, but only present information to the user.

Today's powerful web browsers can do so much that we might tend to lose focus on boundaries. For example, the presentation layer can use AJAX and naturally tends to do some business logic processing with AJAX. However, it is always good practice to stick to the principles.

Summary

In this chapter, we had a look at how we can use the MVC pattern as the basis for separating concerns in the application and assign team members to each layer.

The presentation layer, or the view, is the layer that is most likely to change over time. The business logic layer can also change over time, but not as frequently as the presentation layer. Separating concerns helps us deal with system changes, as the system evolves.

When assigning team members to each layer, and each aspect within a layer, you need to take the personal skills and preferences into account, to ensure team success.

Adhering to the MVC principles will ensure that we can achieve system integration without any major surprises. As long as the model, view, or controller implementations do not cross their boundaries, we can ensure that we have loose coupling in the system, and therefore ensure that we can put them together to get the whole system working seamlessly.

In the next chapter, we will further dive into team allocation concepts and explore key success factors for a PHP software project team.

3
Dealing with Complexity

The MVC pattern helps us cope with the complexity of software systems. Separating concerns based on presentation, business logic, and data makes it easier for us to focus on the specific areas of the software application that we are implementing.

We can design the system adhering to the principles as overtime, when we move deep into the implementation, and when we are busy with the PHP code, the chances of us drifting away from the original design and getting stuck in implementation detail is high. Therefore, rather than trying to implement everything manually from scratch, we should seek the help of tools and frameworks to help us stay on the course, from design to implementation and deployment. Frameworks exist to relieve the programmer so that he can concentrate on project-specific elements like business logic. Therefore, the developers can stay in course with respect to the project, rather than having to bother with technical details that a framework can help with.

In this chapter, we will be covering areas, such as:

- How frameworks simplify the complexity of a project
- Expectations from PHP frameworks
- How to achieve team success with PHP frameworks
- Leading PHP framework examples
- Keeping it all simple with the help of frameworks

Frameworks to simplify complexity

One approach of implementing the MVC pattern is to make sure we identify the PHP classes that fall into each aspect out of the model-view-controller, and then implement each class, ensuring that we do not cross the boundaries. None of the PHP classes should cross over from their respective domains of presentation, business logic processing, and data access. We should stick to well-defined interfaces, when communicating across these layers. The interfacing between the presentation, data, and control layers of the application needs to be defined using proper API documentation. This will help the developers working on each layer to know what to do when it comes to talking to other layers. It is technically possible to do this on our own, when we implement our software system's design using PHP, but needless to say, this requires a considerable amount of engineering effort as well as strict discipline. This approach is also very much error-prone, requiring a considerable amount of time and effort for troubleshooting.

The good news is that over the years, PHP programmers have been dealing with the same problems that I mentioned earlier and have collected their efforts into readily available PHP frameworks. There are plenty of PHP frameworks that support the MVC pattern out of the box.

> A **software framework** provides generic functionality that can be selectively overridden or specialized by user code providing specific functionality. Frameworks provide reusable abstractions of code wrapped in a well-defined API. The overall program's flow of control is dictated by the framework, thereby allowing the developer to focus on domain specific aspects of the software application.

How can frameworks help?

First and foremost, the frameworks simplify the task of dealing with software application complexity. In the first chapter, we discussed how an application grows complex over time, as the application evolves to deal with ever-changing real world requirements. Therefore, the project team would benefit, if they could, from finding a means of dealing with complexity.

The task of adhering to the pattern while implementing the software is a key challenge faced by the software team. Software frameworks simplify this by means of providing a project skeleton. A framework provides us with clear cut separation of the three layers of MVC, so that we will not fall back to crossing the boundaries in our implementation. The framework will also provide us with the interfacing between the three layers, so that we will have little to worry about when integrating the presentation to the business layer and to the data access layer.

When we make use of a framework to implement MVC, the framework will ensure that we will adhere to the design patterns principle on our behalf. We cannot rule out the wrong doing, simply because we are using a framework. However, it makes it difficult to do the incorrect things and makes doing the right thing easier for the team members. The framework in use will ensure that we do not deviate from the correct design. For example, we will not have room to write some PHP code that accesses the database within the controller. Even if we do, we will be able to easily identify that we are doing something wrong, because the framework skeleton will remind us of the correct use of the design pattern.

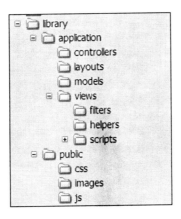

The preceding screenshot shows the Zend Framework's project skeleton for MVC, separating the MVC concerns into different folders.

As the framework guards against deviation from design principles, the use of a framework saves a lot of time. The PHP project team will save the greatest amount of time by not having to worry about integration pains. This is because a framework will ensure the seamless integration of the three layers. Making sure that we do not deviate from the original design also saves a lot of time, because there will not be any additional time spent on syncing up the design with the implementation. Deviating from the intended design causes us to rework. This not only applies to PHP projects, but it also applies to any software project in general. If we cross the boundaries by mixing up presentation and business logic, when it comes to changing the system in the future, in order to facilitate evolution, we would need to spend some considerable time, re-factoring the PHP code to separate the concerns. By using a framework, we can cut down on the need for future refactoring a great deal and just focus on the changes required to improve the system. Therefore, using a framework saves both, time and money.

Frameworks handle complexity on our behalf. The MVC frameworks worry about how to connect to the database and take care of how to manage presentation templates and style sheets. The framework will worry about how to pull data from the data layer and make the data available for the business logic layer. If we were to implement all of these on our own, as PHP developers, we would need to deal with all these complexities. But thanks to all of those developers who implemented the frameworks, we can be relieved from the framework complexities and focus on our data processing, business logic, and how to present information to the user. Therefore, the software project team can focus on the project success and the domain specific aspects of the PHP software project.

There are a few negative sides of using a framework as well. When using a framework, we might not have expert knowledge about the intents of the framework, and therefore, we are merely using it. When we are hit by bugs, it will take time to figure out whether a bug is really in our code or in the framework being used. It will be hard to find solutions to the bugs in the framework itself.

If we are to do fine grained, high performing operations with a framework, we might need to get a deep knowledge to flex the framework into doing what we want. Tuning a framework for performance would be a challenging task, without a great depth of knowledge on the framework.

We might also need to think about licensing problems. With the fine tuning and customization we do with some open source licenses, will need to be contributed back (the business people and company lawyers would not like that idea).

The framework we pick might be either oversized or undersized for the project. We might only use a fraction of the feature set and have a bloated framework on top. On the other hand, we could have a small well-performing frameset that is only capable of doing half of what we need, like different DB interaction and well-performing URL rewriting.

As mentioned in the previous chapter, when implementing a software system, the software team developers need to focus on business logic. This is important to get the system designed and implemented right to solve the problem at hand. If developers are to worry about both the system specific aspect, as well as generic framework aspects, the chances of their focus being deviated are high. Hence, we are better off getting the team to focus on system specific aspects.

Expectations from frameworks

Now that we have discussed how frameworks can help with a PHP project, the next question is what features and capabilities should we look for when choosing a framework. Here are some of the important aspects that we should expect a given PHP framework to support:

- Simple to use
- Facilitates application performance
- Ensures security
- Separates HTML from PHP
- AJAX support
- No restrictions in terms of the PHP constructs that can be used and not having to use custom syntaxes
- An API provided to deal with the framework (object-oriented versus functional)
- Encourages code quality
- Enforces best practices
- Ability to configure
- Supports internationalization
- Availability of comprehensive documentation
- Active community around the framework
- Availability of commercial support
- Friendly license that encourage business use
- No vendor locking
- Availability with web hosting solutions

Based on the nature of the project, not all aspects, but only a subset of the preceding aspects, would be sufficient for our project at hand. For example, internationalization is desired only if we plan to port our application to support multiple languages. But some other aspects, such as simplicity and security, are always desirable. An explanation on each expected aspect of a framework follows. The implication of each aspect on the PHP team project is highlighted in the following discussion.

Simplicity

The PHP framework that we pick for our project needs to facilitate a clean and simple design. The framework should help us keep it simple, rather than making it complex. After all, that is the entire point of using a framework. Though we can assume that frameworks out there would help us simplify the software system that we are to develop, it is always good practice to confirm that it really does. If the steps to get something done with the framework are overly complex, then the project team would not benefit from the use of the framework.

In general, all frameworks provide PHP developers with simplicity, but some frameworks are ahead of the others. Simplicity is always related to the original intent the framework was developed for. Every framework will be simple for those who developed it, because they developed it with certain use cases in mind. If we could stick to those uses, it will be simple. So we need to consciously evaluate the simplicity aspect against our project requirements when making our choice.

The PHP project team will benefit from the simplicity of the framework when it comes to understanding each other's work. It is always good for each team member to have an overall idea about the framework. If the framework is too complicated, it will be challenging for everyone to have the same level of understanding, which will lead towards complications in communication, and sometimes can even be the cause of conflicts among team members.

Size of the framework

One thing that we need to note is that the framework is only part of the solution. We need to implement our own solution based on the framework. If the framework is too bulky, that itself will make our software heavy weight.

It is always desirable for the framework we choose for our project to have a small footprint. A smaller footprint with respect to the amount of memory required, as well as the amount of disk space required is desirable. The number of files has a direct impact on the disk space and governs the file system performance. The size of the files determines the memory required to keep them in memory, as well as the cache memory to handle the file in memory. The number of PHP classes also has an impact on the logical performance. All of these factors contribute to the footprint of the framework. Some frameworks are feature rich, whereas some only have the basics. Based on the nature of our project, we need to evaluate if we are going to use all of the features of the framework that we have chosen. The greater the number of features, the bulkier the framework is going to be.

As a rough measure, you can consider the ratio between the lines of code that we have implemented as part of the project, versus the number of lines of code that is in the framework that we are using. If the PHP framework is much larger than the actual code that we are going to implement as part of the project, maybe we should consider using a smaller framework.

We should always have an idea on the size of the PHP framework that we are using for our project.

Performance

Performance is desirable for any software application. While frameworks provide us with abstract interfaces to help us build our application specific logic, the abstraction layers, if not designed with performance in mind, or if not optimized for performance, can be the cause of system performance bottlenecks. The size of the frameworks is somewhat related to performance. However, size alone does not govern performance.

Similar to the way that the PHP frameworks build on the years of experience with layered web applications, they also improve on performance over time. However, when you evaluate alternatives, when looking for a PHP framework for your project, you need to note that some frameworks will perform better than others. If performance is critical to the nature of our software project, we may need to pay greater attention to performance numbers. The most used criteria for measuring performance is the requests per second measure. Since the end users are working with the presentation layer, you might want to pick a few use cases of your system and load the system with a bunch of requests covering those use cases and evaluate how the framework is performing. This evaluation can be part of the initial **Proof of Concept (POC)** implementation that we might do to evaluate the technical feasibility study of the framework.

Security

Like performance, security is another aspect that any software application needs to take into account. On one hand, the framework itself needs to be secure, guarding against the common security vulnerabilities and protecting against insecure practices, such as allowing the execution of malicious scripts.

On the other hand, the framework helps us write secure code, by providing facilities, such as input validation through filters and a data firewall to guard against SQL injections. We can consciously prevent security vulnerabilities when we are implementing our PHP code. However, the PHP framework being used can prevent us from leaving security holes in our software system.

We need to make sure that team members understand the security features as well as security vulnerabilities, if any, of the PHP framework in use. Also, all of the team members need to be educated on how to use the required security features supported by the framework. Security is one of the areas that we cannot make any assumptions about, and needs to be more precise in terms of instructing and educating team members in this area.

Separate HTML from PHP

When implementing the view, we need to use both PHP as well as HTML. PHP MVC frameworks provide the ability to work with views. However, when maintaining the presentation layer, it is desirable to keep the PHP code in the views extremely simple, and to be able to isolate HTML from PHP logic very easily.

Various frameworks have different strategies when it comes to separating PHP from HTML elements. We need to evaluate these strategies and ensure that the PHP project team can easily work with the PHP and HTML isolation.

AJAX support

Like the HTML and PHP separation, AJAX support is also related to the presentation layer (the view). While it is always possible to use third party libraries for our AJAX usage, it is welcome if the framework can also support AJAX out of the box. That will ensure that the AJAX usage is in sync with the rest of the presentation layer features that come with the framework, and also ensures that we do not go out of the boundaries of the view when using AJAX.

For the project team, it would be an added advantage as the PHP framework will become a one stop shop for the tools that they need to build as comprehensive, dynamic, presentation layer for the application being built. Needing to use a third party library for AJAX on top of the framework, would add the trouble of having to ensure the integration of those libraries with the framework is seamless on our part.

No restrictions

Ideally, the framework that we choose to use for the PHP project should not require us to adhere to restrictive coding rules, especially those that force us to use framework specific markups. The team members are better off if they are not forced to learn a templating language that is specific to a framework.

Though it is highly unlikely that you would want to switch the framework to another in the middle of the project, you always have the chance to use a different PHP framework for the next project. Therefore, it would be a waste of time if the team members had to learn custom coding rules for one framework, and had to throw away that know-how soon after the project finishes. It is always welcome to use generic HTML, AJAX, and, most importantly, PHP syntaxes when implementing the software application.

It saves time, in terms of getting up to speed with the project, if there are no restrictions or custom rules required by the framework, because the project team can make use of the PHP knowledge, which they already have, to get going with the project right from the beginning. Otherwise, they would need to spend a considerable amount of time studying the framework before the start of the project.

Object-oriented versus functional

Some frameworks supports object-oriented APIs, while others provide functional APIs. Most of the PHP projects these days use object-oriented designs. Therefore, if the project wants to use an object-oriented implementation and the framework does not support it, it might lead to problems. Project team members especially will find it difficult to sync up the use of the framework and custom code that they are implementing if the framework supports a different style of programming to that used by the custom logic. Therefore, based on the fact that we are either using object-oriented programming or functional programming, we need to consider the programming styles supported by the PHP framework that we are going to use.

We should make sure that all of the team members feel comfortable with the API provided by the PHP framework, and that they are familiar with the style of the API. For the sake of maintaining the project in the long run, we are better off using a framework that supports an object-oriented programming style, as object orientation is supposed to help with some maintenance headaches.

Code quality of the project

Code quality is critical to any software system that is developed by a team of people. Not only those who have written a given piece of code, but also others in the project team need to be able to look into that piece of code to understand what is it doing.

When using a framework, the code quality of the programmers can be improved and sometimes enforced by the framework itself. For example, the framework can avoid layers and other complexities to make the code easier to audit. The framework can help the programmers to minimize code and help team members avoid repeating their work.

However, it is not possible for the framework to enforce something like a coding standard for the code that we implement on top of the framework. Therefore, we need to keep in mind, that it is the responsibility of the team to adhere to a coding standard. It is always a good practice to have a coding standard defined for the project so that the project team can follow that. Also, it is always a good idea to sync up the coding standard with the framework (for example, if there are situations that the framework can auto generate code).

Coding standards are a set of guidelines for a specific programming language that recommend programming style, practices, and methods for each aspect of a piece program written in this language. These conventions usually cover file organization, indentation, comments, declarations, statements, white space, and naming conventions.

For example: Drupal Coding Standards (http://drupal.org/coding-standards)

Enforce best practices

The framework that we use can help enforce best practices that we want our PHP project team to follow. Code quality is about writing neat code. A good practice is to use programming constructs that ensure the ideal use of technology, when implementing various technical aspects of the software project.

A **best practice** is a technique, method, process, or activity that is more effective at delivering a particular outcome than any other technique, method, or process. The key idea is that with proper processes, checks, and testing, a desired outcome can be delivered with fewer problems and unforeseen complications.

For example, security, authentication, database access, and session handling are common technical aspects that we need to worry about in any software project. There are various patterns and practices that we can leverage when dealing with these technicalities. PHP frameworks can provide us with programming constructs to help us better deal with these technical aspects, without compromising the quality of the software that we are implementing.

For example, we can devise our own mechanisms to deal with application state. However, the PHP framework that we use can help us deal with application state, with the help of managed sessions. Rather than reinventing the wheel, we can benefit from the features provided by the framework. And, more importantly, when using the session feature of the framework, it will enforce us to adhere to best practices with respect to management of sessions. For example, the sessions need to expire after some time, and the framework would handle that for us.

Another example is the use of connection pools when accessing databases. The framework can manage the connection pool on our behalf, and we will be using the best practice of reusing connections.

Like with the case of sessions and connection pools, there can be many best practices that will be enforced by the PHP framework that we are going to use for our project. We need to educate the project team members of those best practices, so they always look to benefit from them. And, more importantly, when they are educated of those best practices, they will reuse that knowledge on future projects as well.

Configuration needs

PHP frameworks often provide configuration options. Some configuration elements are common to the entire framework (for example, where the required include files are located). Some other configuration elements are application specific (for example, database connection parameters for the application).

While configuration abstracts out common concerns, too many configuration needs can also lead to complications. Therefore, the PHP frameworks nowadays try to achieve zero or no configuration.

Convention over Configuration is a software design paradigm, which seeks to decrease the number of decisions that developers need to make, gaining simplicity, but without sacrificing flexibility. This paradigm is also known as Coding by Convention. The framework most strongly associated with the paradigm is Ruby (a programming language) on Rails (http://www.rubyonrails.org/), which popularized the concept.

We need to verify if the framework needs only simple configuration that can be achieved with a few simple steps and with, at most, one configuration file. If it requires more than one configuration file, it always leads to maintenance headaches — especially in an environment where a team of people work on the project. Also, you need to make sure in the development phase that if one member changes the configurations with respect to the PHP framework in use, then the others get to know of those changes as soon as possible. Otherwise, if the changes to the configuration affect the entire system, but other team members do not get to know the changes, others will be testing their implementations against an expired configuration. Therefore, changes to the configurations need to be dealt with care, like the way you might deal with major API changes that affect the entire system. For example, either the changes need to be communicated to everyone in the team through email, or configuration files need to be shared with a source control system.

Internationalization

If we want to support more than one human language with our application, we need to make sure that we do not hard code anything in a particular language (for example, in English) in the presentation layer. In case we want to internationalize the application, the usual way of supporting that is to use some key in the presentation layer, and provide the mapping to that key, in a language specific property file. Form headings, labels, alert messages, and so on will all have a key used in the property file, instead of real wording, and the framework will take care of picking the correct mapping and rendering the expected language when sending the response to web browser requests.

When we are choosing a framework for our PHP project, if internationalization is a project requirement, it would be ideal for the framework to support internationalization as an inherent feature. If the framework does not support internationalization, we will be able to use another third party library to get the job done.

When we are using internationalization features of the framework, we need to train the team members working on the project on how to adhere to internationalization requirements. In particular, the regular mode of programming is to have all of the text in PHP or HTML files. Therefore, the sub-team working on the presentation layer needs to be disciplined in use of the property files for text, and replace text in PHP or HTML files with respective keys. Another thing to note is that it is not only the presentation layer sub-team who should be aware of the expectations for internationalization. Sometimes, the content presented through the presentation layer comes from the backend, the business logic layer. So if internationalization is in use, those who work on the business layer need to be aware of it too, so that they can apply internationalization rules when providing content to the front end.

When we are programming, we can use one property file, and use the language that we are familiar with, rather than worrying about maintaining multiple language mapping property files. Once the system is implemented, we can use the single property file and translate that to the other languages.

Documentation

Often, we get too excited about the feature set provided by a PHP framework and tend to overlook the need for documentation. We do this until we hit a road block with the project, where we might need to go through the framework's code to understand how to do something. Almost all frameworks will come with documentation. However, some frameworks will stand out from others, in that they provide clear, thorough, and comprehensive documentation.

Rather than taking documentation for granted, we need to make it a point to look into the documentation of the framework, and determine if that covers the breadth of features, in depth, in the documentation. Sometimes, the framework will be designed in such a manner that experienced programmers could use their intuition to understand the API and get the job done. However, not all members in your team will be that experienced. Someone who runs into a problem when implementing a niche feature of the project should have somewhere to look, and documentation is the best resort. Therefore, we need to make sure that the documentation does really help, rather than only touch the surface.

One of the pitfalls when evaluating documentation is to mix up the availability of a large number of samples to the equivalent of good documentation. Samples are always helpful and welcome. However, for the samples to become really useful, there should be accompanying documentation. Ideally, each sample should have associated documentation.

We should encourage the team members to look into documentation, especially at the beginning of the project, if they are not familiar with the framework to be used for the PHP project. A framework's documentation needs to be a key part of the project knowledge base.

Community

Documentation, when necessary, is nothing next to lively human interactions. Also, it is not possible to document all possible scenarios supported by a framework. There can be situations where we need to get something done with the framework, but the application that we are developing using the PHP framework is so unique, that few people have even tried to do the same with the framework before. In such a situation, it would be a luxury to get someone with better expertise on the framework to help you.

More often than not, the framework of our choice will be an open source PHP framework. Given that the core PHP engine itself is open source, it does not make sense to use a proprietary framework based on PHP as the base of our PHP application. Open source projects are driven by communities. There will be a developer community, as well as one or more user communities associated with an open source PHP framework. The advantage of having a strong community behind the PHP framework of our choice is that we will be able to get help for the problems that we face with the framework. Maybe they have already seen the same problem, and figured out a workaround or found a solution. Maybe they have better knowledge and experience with the framework than us, allowing them to shed some light as to how to proceed with the framework in search of a solution to the problem that we have faced.

The communities behind a PHP framework can use various channels, such as email lists, online forums, and even IRC channels.

Some communities are really active, where you might get your questions answered within hours. Some communities can be really friendly, willing to help you get over the problems, and even tolerate seemingly silly questions on the part of the dummy users. However, some communities might not be that active, and sometimes, even though they are active, they might not be that friendly towards newbies. Therefore, when you select a framework for your project, it is better to consider the possibility of your team members getting some help in case they run into trouble with the communities. Look into the history of the forums, and mailing list archives of the PHP framework that will be chosen for the project, to evaluate the activeness as well as the friendliness of the community.

The other important aspect of an active community behind a PHP framework is that someone might have faced the kind of question that you have faced. There is a chance that someone has already asked the question that you wanted to ask from the community, and someone has already answered that question. In other words, we can treat the forum history and mailing list archive of the framework to be an informal documentation on the framework. We can ask the project team members to dig into the community archives in search of answers to the problems that they face. However, this is only feasible if there is a considerable amount of history of archived community communications. Therefore, it would be a good idea to include this as one of the evaluation criteria when selecting a PHP framework for your project.

Commercial support

As it was mentioned while discussing the community aspect, we would hardly choose a PHP framework that is non-open source for our PHP project. However, there can be situations where we might run into bugs in the framework itself, other than bugs on our own code. In such situations, we might be able to depend on the user and developer communities around the framework, to help us to overcome the problem. However, this help comes purely on a voluntary basis. In other words, no one in any of the communities is liable to provide a solution to a potential bug that we might find in the framework. And even if they did, we cannot guarantee that we might be able to find a solution within the time frame that we desire, in case we are up against a tight deadline in terms of our project. The solution for this sort of uncertainty is to look for commercial support offered around the PHP framework that we are using.

Commercial support provides us with insurance against potential show-stoppers when we are using a framework. Commercial support can come in many forms; training, development support, and production support. Development support is where the organization providing commercial support provides us with support for the problems that we hit while developing our project. Even though we might already have a training package, the chances are good that the training will not cover the unique situations that we come across while working on our project. Therefore, while working on our project, we might want to seek help from the experts on the framework that we are using. So, development support is to get help as and when needed, while developing the project using the framework. Production support is the insurance package that we purchase against potential showstoppers that we hit once we deploy the software that we have developed. If the bug that breaks the live system happens to be one in the framework, we would rather get the experts to fix that rather than trying to handle them on our own. This is because of the business impact it will have on the live system is down for a prolonged time. Out of those options, production support might be the most important as training and development support would be redundant, based on the expertise of our team members.

You need to remember that you should look for commercial support only if it is absolutely necessary. Most small to medium projects would not have a big enough budget to go for a third party support model. If your project is large scale and the application is mission critical in terms of the business value that the application yields to the organization, it will be beneficial to have some insurance in the form of commercial support. In case the community behind the framework is active and regularly releases the framework, which minimizes the need for commercial support even if there are bugs, there is a chance that they would get fixed soon. However, unless we ourselves participate in the development aspects of the framework, we cannot guarantee that the bugs would be fixed in the next release of the framework.

Also, remember that even though the framework will be an open source product, it would not be a good idea to customize it on our own. This is because when the next release comes up, we would have trouble integrating our local custom changes to the framework's new code. Therefore, if we have done bug fixes to the framework on our own, it would be a good idea to donate them back to the development community of the framework. This way, those fixes will be available in the next release and we would not have trouble upgrading to the next release. The importance of upgrading to a newer release is that there would be many bug fixes from the previous release to the new release. And the good thing about donating the fixes that we do is that we would be giving something back in gratitude to all of the hard work that the developer community has done while implementing the framework. It would build a good relationship between our project team and the framework's development and user communities.

If we are looking to help fix a bug that we have found, a less costly model compared to full-scale commercial production support is the development sponsorship. It means that we pay an individual or group just to fix the particular bugs that we desperately want fixed in the framework. It saves time on our part, as we are not spending any of our team members' time to fix framework bugs. Also, we can get experts who know how to fix the framework, rather than wasting our team members' time to learn how to fix the framework. They would be able to get the fix quickly.

Even if you do not plan to purchase commercial support due to budgetary constraints, it would be useful to pick a PHP framework that provides commercial support in some form. This leaves you the option of using paid support, in case your project team runs into a crisis situation in the future. A framework with commercial support options should score more marks over those that do not offer that option, when we are evaluating our alternatives.

License

Open source PHP frameworks will come with some form of an open source license. We must pay attention to the license of the PHP framework that we are going to use for our project, because the kind of license has some business implications. Not only should the organization that we work for feel comfortable with the license, but also the clients who are going to use the software that we develop will be interested in the license.

Determining whether the license suits the software project at hand is a very subjective matter. More often than not, it is not the software project team, but rather the company lawyers who need to decide on the licensing matters. Therefore, it would be advisable to consult relevant parties on the kind of license that the framework uses, before the start of the project. If we happen to find out that the license does not suit the business objectives of the project, half way down the line in project life cycle, we might need to throw away all of the hard technical work that we have done. Therefore, we should make it a point to look into the license as one of the first evaluation criteria of the PHP framework that we are going to use.

Some organizations have well-defined guidelines on getting a license approved. Sometimes there can be a subset of licenses approved already by the organization to be used in projects. If we have already used the framework for one project, we might not be able to assume that the same framework could be used for the next project, as the client of the new project might have different aspirations when it comes to legal matters. Therefore, always make sure to double-check the license, before the start of the project.

Sometimes, there could be concerns over the **intellectual property (IP)** implications. The main question to be asked here is, 'who developed this software framework?'. Some PHP frameworks are developed by a few individuals and some are by larger teams. We might need to look into the copyright claims, and verify that there aren't any IP violations.

Vendor locking

Sometimes, a framework could seem to have great set of features, but only part of that would be available as open source. If we happen to start the project using a particular framework, and somewhere down the line when we feel the need of a particular feature, but that is only available without paid support, we would have no other option but to pay for it. However, the same feature would be available with another framework for free. Now if we want to switch from the first framework, to this other framework that we found to be more liberal, we should be able to do that. If the first framework's coding and configuration style prevented us doing the migration easily, and we had to continue using the same framework, that is vendor locking. Now we need to keep on using the same framework and adhere to the terms of framework, whether we like it or not. We should try and avoid vendor locks at all costs.

It is a fact that we cannot switch from one framework to another seamlessly, without doing changes. However, we should be able to get our custom code migrated, with comparatively little effort, if the need arises. These kinds of unpleasant and complicated changes can be avoided through proper evaluation of the framework at the start of the project. We should look for possible vendor locking opportunities in a PHP framework and try and avoid using such frameworks for our PHP project.

Availability with hosting

Most PHP projects, once developed and completed, will be required to be deployed with a web hosting service provider. Standard hosting accounts run a variety of PHP versions and configurations. The framework that we choose as the base of our PHP project should be compatible with those that the standard hosting accounts provide.

Some PHP frameworks will be made available by the web hosting companies themselves, reducing the hassle of installing and configuring those frameworks. If the framework we chose is not readily available from the hosting company that we want, we should be able to install and configure the framework easily.

Although the chances that will we switch between frameworks over time for a project is minimal, the chances that we might need to change our web hosting provider over time is greater. Therefore, we should consider the availability and support of the framework with multiple web hosting companies, when we choose a framework.

Some more points to ponder

In addition to the above facts that need to be taken into account when evaluating PHP frameworks, here are some more points that will be helpful to evaluate the usefulness of the PHP framework to be used for the PHP project.

The PHP framework should support multiple databases. Often, we pick a database management system for the project and stick with it. However, due to various constraints such as security, performance, and license, we might want to switch between database management systems. So it would be useful for the PHP framework to support multiple databases.

Support for **Object Relational Mapping (ORM)** by the PHP framework is also going to be very useful when it comes to the style of development. The PHP developers will benefit a great deal by not having to deal with low level SQL, but with objects using ORM, which is natural to programming. This also increases developer productivity.

Support for templates is a welcome feature by the framework. We discussed how the templates help in the previous chapter. The kind of template support that the PHP framework provides will have a great impact on the way we deal with our presentation layer.

Support for modules, including authentication modules, is another handy feature to have in the PHP framework. In the previous chapter, we discussed the need for having a unified model for cross-cutting concerns such as security. And we can rely on the PHP framework to help us with these cross-cutting concerns. For example, the authentication module of the PHP framework can ensure that we address authentication in a consistent manner throughout our application.

Team success with frameworks

In the above sections, we looked in detail at each desired aspect of a PHP framework. For a team to be successful with a framework, they should feel comfortable with the framework and they should consider the framework to help the teamwork, rather than hinder their team effort. Sometimes, to ensure that the team has a positive attitude towards the PHP framework being used for the project, all that is required is to set a positive tone among team members right at the beginning of the project.

Different team members that have worked with various PHP frameworks might have developed various feelings and attitudes towards the framework that they have used. Some of these feelings might be subjective rather than objective, and these feelings could lead to political battles among team members to prove that one framework is better than the other. This will damage the team unity, as well as we might not be able to achieve the project goals, if members try to keep on proving their points. Therefore, we might need to do a proper objective evaluation of the alternative frameworks available at the beginning of the project, and educate all team members on the objective rationales for choosing the framework to be used for the project. Once the choice is made, the team better uses it in completion, rather than keep on arguing on the possible alternatives.

One other key aspect is that people take pride in what they do. This is very important in terms of a software team. Each member should feel that they do something that makes them valuable over time. The experience that they gain and things that they learn by working on a project, using some framework, should motivate them. If the framework being used for the project is in wide use in the industry, the software team might feel more comfortable working with that because they would have some sense of job security. If we are using a framework that is not widely used in the industry, team members might be concerned if it will be really useful to learn how to use that, with respect to their future opportunities to use the same framework in the future.

The current experience that various team members have on the framework being used for the project can also come in handy for the success of the project. Those members with experience can educate, guide, and help others in the team to make better use of the framework. It is always a good idea to have some experts, or geeks, with respect to the framework in use, as they can prevent the entire project from hitting roadblocks and showstoppers.

As we discussed in the previous chapter, we can allocate team members based on presentation, business, and data layers. We can also take into account the level of experience that each team member has on the framework, when allocating team members to various work items.

It is also important to note that we need to educate the team on various aspects with respect to the use of the framework. The usual approach is to assume that the PHP project team will make good use of the project. However, it is not a good idea to assume the proper use and expect great results. We need to first make sure that we explicitly educate the developers in terms of the proper use of the framework, and what we expect from the use of the framework. It is also important to highlight various aspects as were discussed in the previous sections, based on the importance of those aspects to the project we are working on. In addition to educating team members, we should also monitor the use of framework by the team members and evaluate results, to ensure that we are on right path, throughout the project. Regular reviews will help us stay on course, throughout the project life cycle.

Technical feasibility study of the framework

We have discussed the various aspects that we wish to have and use in the PHP framework for the project at hand. Most of these aspects have some elements that need to be highlighted with respect to the project team. At the start of the project, we should do a technical feasibility study, on the PHP framework to be used for the project and the elements that have implications of the project team should also be evaluated.

Sometimes, if we have already used the PHP framework for several projects already, we might be inclined to skip the technical evaluation as we are already familiar with the framework. However, no matter how familiar we are with the framework, we should not skip the technical feasibility study for a new project. This is because every time we get a new project, the technical and business requirements of that project are unique and cannot be compared to any of the previous projects that we have already completed. In fact, if the new project is identical to any of the projects that we have done earlier, it would not be a new project as such. Therefore, if we are to succeed with the new project, we need to do a technical feasibility against the framework that we plan to use for the project and be confident about the technical fitness of that framework for the project at hand.

People factor is an important element in the technical feasibility evaluation, but it is often overlooked. It is critical that we consider the current experience of the team members on the framework to be used if they would feel comfortable with the style of programming offered by the framework. If we cannot align the technical aspirations of the project team to the nature of the framework, we will face hardships during project life cycle.

PHP Frameworks

Here is a list of a few leading PHP frameworks that you might consider evaluating for your project.

Limb

URL: `http://limb-project.com/`

Open source with GNU LGPL license.

Limb is mostly aimed for rapid web application, prototyping, and development. Limb is a library that consists of many reusable components distributed as packages. This allows us to pick the components that we need and combine them with other frameworks and libraries, such as ZendFramework, Symfony, PEAR, and so on.

It includes a package named `macro`, a powerful and highly customizable templating system that uses user-defined macro tags for the presentation layer. The `web_app` package provides a FrontController interface, which handles the controller responsibilities of the MVC pattern. The package named `dbal` provides the database abstraction layer, which currently supports MySql, PostreSQL, Oracle, and SQLite.

To help evaluate Limb in action, there is a **Code Bits** section where code samples, as well as applications built on this framework, can be found.

phpDrone

URL: `http://www.phpdrone.cvds.ro/`

Open source with custom license.

phpDrone requires at least PHP5 or a higher version. The main features of phpDrone are:

- An advanced templating system for presentation layer
- A controller module that will map the URL to methods inside your PHP code, and handles controller responsibilities of MVC
- A set of widgets (for example, HTML form widget for easy handling of HTML forms)

phpDrone has the latest documentation in the **Docs** section of their site.

ZNF

URL: `http://www.zeronotice.org/`

Open source with GNU LGPL license.

The goal of ZNF is to provide a framework for building PHP5 enterprise web applications. The core of the ZNF framework is a flexible control layer based on standard technologies like PHP5 and XML. ZNF encourages application architectures based on the Model 2 approach, a variation of the MVC design paradigm.

ZNF provides its own controller component. This controller component integrates with other technologies to provide the model and the view.

For implementing the model, the data layer—ZNF—can interact with standard data access technologies, like PEAR::MDB2 and PDO.

ATK

URL: `http://www.atk-framework.com/`

Open source with GNU LGPL license.

ATK is a framework targeted at business applications. It promises very small amounts of code, when building applications.

The philosophy behind ATK is to archive minimal code, eliminate code duplication, simplicity, and reuse. With this view, the key idea is to ensure that the only code the user writes is business logic. There is a comprehensive demonstration to help us understand this concept. Also note that ATK claims that it is not a component framework. Therefore, the approach is slightly different form traditional frameworks.

Akelos

URL: `http://www.akelos.org/`

Open source with GNU LGPL license.

The Akelos PHP Framework is an MVC framework. It provides comprehensive support to build applications based on MVC design pattern.

Akelos provides AJAX support for views. The controller handles requests and responses on behalf of the user. It provides a simple mapping between models and the databases.

Akelos also has internationalization support.

Akelos claims that it can run applications on most shared hosting service providers since it only requires PHP to be available on the server.

CakePHP

URL: `http://www.cakephp.org/`

Open source with MIT license.

CakePHP is a rapid development framework for PHP. It has the provision to use MVC within the convention over configuration paradigm, and eliminates the need for configuration requirements. CakePHP also promises less code.

CakePHP defines a comprehensive set of best practices covering security, authentication, and session handling.

The framework provides an object-oriented API for the programmers to work with.

CodeIgniter

URL: `http://codeigniter.com/`

Open source with custom license.

CodeIgniter is a PHP framework with a very small footprint. Because of the small footprint, good performance can also be expected. CodeIgniter also promises wide support for shared hosting accounts. One of the most interesting features of CodeIgniter is that it does not require a custom templating language.

Thorough documentation is available.

Zend Framework

URL: `http://framework.zend.com/`

Open source with New BSD license.

Zend Framework is based on simplicity, object-oriented best practices and a rigorously tested agile code base. Zend Framework is focused on building more secure, reliable, and modern Web 2.0 applications.

Zend Framework has comprehensive MVC support, with clear separation between the presentation, business logic, and data access layers. It also has support for AJAX for the presentation layer. It also has support for web services and data syndication formats. You can use those as an alternative to your database driven data model.

In addition to the MVC support, Zend Framework comes with a comprehensive object-oriented PHP 5 class library. It has paid proper attention to best practices like design patterns, unit testing, and loose coupling in the design of the framework and the API.

PHP Work

URL: `http://www.phpwork.org/`

Open source with MIT license.

PHP Work too is a MVC framework. It tries to closely follow architecture similar to ASP.NET. It provides clear separation between presentation logic and business logic through its approach for web page organizing.

It makes extensive use of object-oriented concepts.

Symfony

URL: `http://www.symfony-project.org/`

Open source with custom license.

Symfony is a comprehensive framework based on PHP5. It provides an architecture, components, and tools, for developers to build complex web applications. It makes use of the best practices of web development by integrating some third-party libraries.

Symfony is one of the most popular PHP5 frameworks around. Therefore, there is a large community behind it. This makes it very easy to find help, documentation, and plugins.

You can find a comprehensive comparison of the PHP frameworks and a summary table comparing some leading frameworks at `http://www.phpframeworks.com/`. In the above section, the PHP frameworks discussed were picked based on the level of MVC support they provide. While almost any PHP framework supports MVC, each framework has its own approach.

KISS—beyond frameworks

Using a PHP framework, we can delegate the complexity of dealing with the flow of control. In the section above, we discussed in detail what to look for when selecting a framework, what to expect out of a framework, and how we should organize our team to get the maximum use out of the framework.

Most of the concepts we discussed with respect to the PHP frameworks can be generalized to any tool or library that we plan to use for our PHP project. For example, we always need to look into the documentation, samples, and community support of any piece of software that we are going to use for the project, because the team members working on the project need technical support. Based on the budget available, the project management might even decide to look for commercial support. Also, the company lawyers are interested in the kind of license under which the libraries that we are going to use.

Beyond frameworks

We know for sure that frameworks will help us simplify our projects. However, frameworks alone cannot help. In other words, it is not only about frameworks. Frameworks will simplify, but we need to KISS.

 KISS is an acronym for **Keep it Short and Simple**, and sometimes it is also used to mean a more popular term **Keep it Simple, Stupid**. KISS states that design simplicity should be a key goal and that unnecessary complexity should be avoided.

When designing the software application, we cannot leave any responsibility to the framework or any other tools that we might be using, when it comes to the quality of the software design. Most people are good at complex designs, but often overlook the need for maintenance. It is the logic that we implement on top of the framework, the application specific logic, that is most important. We need to make that implementation simple to manage complexity.

The thumb rule that we can follow, when it comes to the KISS principle, is to do the least possible to meet the requirements. In other words, we need to avoid over design. One way of achieving this is to encourage and reward simple design over complex solutions done by team members. Our application logic that we implement on top of the PHP framework in use needs to be as simple and clean as PHP.

People are complex

People are the most complex element in a software project. When we talk about a team, we are basically talking about a set of people working as a team.

Usually, the team members are motivated, even more, by exploring and learning new things. This is especially true about software professionals. They will be less motivated to fix bugs and write test cases, than to implement some new logic. We need to manage those traits of individuals to get the project done right. From a project perspective, not only new logic, but also the bug fixes and test cases matter. Therefore, we need to balance out the task assignments and responsibilities.

Avoid NIH

Not Invented Here (NIH) is a term used to describe corporate or institutional culture that avoids using or buying already existing products, research, or knowledge because of its different origins. Sometimes, some team members will not want to use a framework feature, tool, or library, due to this mindset.

It is important to get team members to reuse everything around, at all costs. This will solve the problems with writing too much new code, requiring rigorous testing, and sometimes leading to overly complicated software. We should not only try and reuse the features offered by the PHP framework that we are using, but also, we need to reuse the code that our own team members have implemented.

Innovation

Many have the misconception that innovation is about coming up with something, out of the blue. However, all great innovations around us were built by just improving what was already around. This phenomenon applies to software projects as well. The entire point of using a PHP framework is to make sure that we are not trying to reinvent the wheel. But at the same time, based on the framework that we are going to use, there is so much room to innovate.

The clients and the stakeholders of the PHP project that we undertake have some problem at hand. We can put our imagination to work just by looking at the current solutions they have and by building on top of those.

Embrace change

Throughout the project life cycle, you will need to deal with changes. Even if you are using a framework today, if we hit a technical roadblock due to some policy or strategy change at the top, we might need to switch the framework. Now that is a drastic change. However, we have to change the selected framework.

There is nothing permanent except change – Heraclitus

One fundamental solution to the problem of changing requirements is to be ready to accept the change requests and be willing to change. If we have designed the system in such a way that the system cannot be changed, or if we did change and everything comes crashing down, then it is going to be a serious problem. No one designs the application to be immutable by intent. But the system gets larger as the project progresses, and the software becomes big and messy, making it fragile.

While we need to keep our system design simple, we also need to make the system tolerable to changes. Though it sounds complex to design a system to tolerate change, we can achieve this by following a few principles. Things as simple as the use of a coding convention, use of constants instead of hard coded values, and separation of concerns will lead us to deal with changes better.

The other most intriguing factor when it comes to dealing with change is the resistance to change on the part of the team members. In this aspect too, nothing could help more than education.

Simplicity is a mindset

The secret of success, when it comes to dealing with complexity, is to have the mindset of simplicity. The coding discipline, the team iterations, approach towards design, use of tools, use of libraries, use of frameworks, assignment of team members, all should be done with simplicity in mind.

The rationale is that, we as human being find it very difficult to deal with complex problems and complex systems. But unfortunately, today's software realities ends with us building very complex and complicated systems. We need to break down the problems, make use of existing knowledge, and tools on software, and try to break down the complexity into simple and manageable small elements. That will help us to succeed with our PHP team projects.

Summary

Implementing a pattern such as MVC manually, without a framework, requires a great deal of engineering effort and time, and is also more error-prone. Therefore, we will benefit a great deal from the use of a PHP framework.

When looking for a PHP framework for our project, there are various aspects that we need to worry about. We need to make sure that those aspects are up to satisfaction, with respect to the project at hand.

Both technical aspects, as well as team and human aspects, need to be taken into account when evaluating a framework for our project. Educating the team with respect to expectations, requirements, and technical aspects in relation to the project and the framework to be used for the project will be a key factor that governs the project success.

Simplicity is the most significant principle when it comes to designing and implementing the project. We need to keep focus on the project-specific implementation that we do on top of the framework, and ensure that we adhere to simplicity principles to guarantee that we can manage and maintain the PHP project in the long run. Each team member needs to consciously contribute to keep the project simple and deal with complexities.

4
The Process Matters

If we are to succeed with anything that we do as we go along, the way we do it matters a lot. For example, our ability to pass an examination depends on the way we follow the course, attend the coursework, read the additional material, and study for the exam, from the day we start attending classes for the subject. This phenomenon applies to software development as well. People often look at the software application, in other words the product, and judge the quality of the software. However, the fact is often overlooked that the kind of process that is used to develop the software has a major impact on the quality of the software that is delivered.

In this chapter, we will look into the importance of the process for PHP projects. Even though PHP projects seem to be simple, as discussed in the first chapter, today's enterprise applications, which are developed using PHP, demand discipline and a systematic approach for the projects to be successful.

In this chapter, we will discuss:

- The relationship between the process and the product
- Consequences of ignoring the process
- Why the process must be respected
- Moving from no process to some process
- Process helps, not hinder
- A simple process for PHP projects

Process and product

In the software engineering discipline, the process takes center stage when it comes to developing software. One of the key objectives of the use of a process model in software engineering is to ensure that we can predict the time and effort required for the software being developed. The process aims to cut down the number of bugs, increase developer productivity, and improve the quality of the software being developed.

 The quality of a software application defines its ability to fit the purpose that the software is being used for. Quality is the ability of the software application to meet the needs of its users.

If we adhere to good practices in our process, the possibility of ending up with a high quality product is very high. In other words, the quality of the product is governed by the quality of the process.

The key challenges faced when ensuring product quality includes our ability to meet user expectations, reducing the number of bugs, ensuring that we can accommodate changes in requirements, and guaranteeing quality aspirations such as security and usability. In theory, user requirements and user expectations are identical. However, we need to understand that the user will have trouble explaining the expectations precisely. Therefore, there can be a gap between what we capture as user requirements and what the user expects in the back of their minds.

The kind of process we have can help us deal with these challenges. For example, if the process facilitate regular deliverables in shorter time intervals, it becomes easy to get the user to evaluate those and incorporate the user feedback into the product effectively. Incorporating user feedback makes sure the product we develop better fits the user's purpose. If the process facilitates regular reviews, we can ensure that bugs are found earlier and hence, over time, we would be able to cut down the bug rate drastically.

In a PHP software project, the quality of the application being developed can be hindered by the violations with respect to the application of the MVC model. In each layer of the MVC model there can be various mistakes that could lead to various quality problems. For example, in the view, there can be inconsistencies among various forms and reports with respect to where the action buttons are placed and how the columns of reports are laid out. These kind of inconsistencies can lead to a great deal of usability problems and the end users can tend to think that the system is of low quality.

One other main problem related to presentation would be the lack of data used in forms or reports. The root cause for such a situation would be the fact that a proper technique was not used to capture what the user really wanted. For example, we need to sit with the users and try to fully capture what they want to see in a report and what they want to capture with a form. If, as developers, we make assumptions on what the users might want, the chances are that we might not be able to capture what the user really wanted. Collaborating with the user is the key to understanding what they really want.

Sometimes, users might find out that the application did not do what they wanted it to do. Often, developers could get carried away by the technology and elegance of the application's architecture. Those aspects are important for an application. However, in enterprise applications, the most important aspect is to make the application **fit for purpose**. Irrespective of the fact that the application is technically superior, it needs to help users to get the job (that they want out of it) done.

 A software process is the set of activities that produces a software product. Each activity will have an associated result. When those results, from each activity, are put together in some defined order, it will result in a software product.

If we have a process in place, it should guard us against slipping out of the quality aspirations of the application being developed. Inconsistencies, not only in UI, but also in all aspects (such as the APIs of the interfacing layers) can be avoided with the help of a process that the team follows. For example, we can define the expected consistency guidelines for the user interface, and through the process, we can define steps for the team members to follow. This would ensure that they would follow the set guidelines. They can refer to the guidelines before attending to a task, while designing the UI, and after the implementation is done. There can be review sessions to verify the implementation against the guidelines. The idea here is not to define a set of rules that the team members follow while working on the project, but rather to let them know what to be done, in case they want to ensure high quality outcomes form what they do. In other words, guidelines are not rules, rather they are advice on how to do things right. The team members can learn from them and build on top of those, and at times, even go to the extent of improving the guidelines themselves.

The process could enforce that we capture the user story using some tools, before we design and implement that. It is easy to get a very high level picture of what the users want and jump into implementation, especially with PHP. However, in a well-defined process, the input for the design and implementation phase for a user story would be a well-documented user story captured by analyzing what the users want. This ensures that we meet the user's expectations in completion rather than partially, and users will admire the software that we develop to be of high quality.

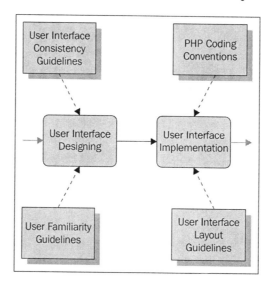

When designing user interfaces for forms and reports, we can use story boards to ensure that we capture the requirements properly. Given the simplicity of the PHP language and its ability to facilitate a simple implementation in quick time, we can rapidly build some prototypes. This way, we will get the user feedback sooner, before we jump into real implementation.

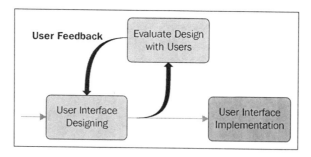

Software processes simplify our lives by ensuring that we do not miss some trivial activities, which introduce some good practices on our path to implementing a good product. Sometimes, developers tend to treat a process to be something that is burdening the free flow of design and implementation. Of course we can, and we should, make the process simple and fun to follow for developers. This is especially true when a programming language as simple and powerful as PHP is in use. But at the same time, the importance of a process in place should not be overlooked.

The article that can be found at `http://www.tonymarston.net/php-mysql/ infrastructure.html`, titled, A Development Infrastructure for PHP, discusses a basic framework that can be a useful reference for your PHP project.

Ignoring the process

With a powerful scripting language, such as PHP, the individual development tasks of a project can be very simple. When the complex system is broken down into smaller, simpler tasks, the usual temptation is to not see the complete picture. Therefore, the individual team members will not see any rationale for a systematic approach for doing things that are too simple and trivial.

Over-simplification of the tasks at hand can be life threatening when it comes to a serious PHP project. If the project is not serious, you do not need an organized team anyway. It is true that we should divide the overall complex problem into smaller manageable parts. However, that should not lead to a situation where the team members are misinterpreting simplicity. If the task is so trivial, let it be so and do not try to make it complex. However, always think of the overall picture of the entire project. We need to always take into account the fact that there are other members of the team working on the other parts of the project, the view, the controller, and the model. We need to make an effort to be in sync with the rest of the team and ensure that all individual pieces of the puzzle, which the team is working on, fit together. It is the process that helps us to be consistent across and to be in sync with each other. Overlooking the process due to perceived simplification of the individual pieces of the puzzle can lead to project failure.

As mentioned at the end of the previous section, developers usually tend to treat the process as a reason for slowing things down. It is far easier to just work on the code and skip all of the formalities around. Doing a quick and dirty hack makes sure that the system is up and running and gets over that nasty bug, and it is required to do so at times.

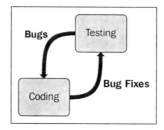

However, the most important aspect that we need to keep in mind is the fact that we work in a team. The dirty fix that gets over one bug, might introduce several new ones. In the context of software engineering, regression is a bug which makes a feature stop functioning as intended. Regression can also break what others have done and what others are planning to do. Therefore, if an API is hacked to work for one case it might break many other cases. How can we prevent this sort of regression? The process is supposed to help here. If you follow the process that should guard against regression. If the process does not do that, we need to fix the process, to ensure that it helps us to keep the project on track.

The article located at `http://qa.php.net/write-test.php`, discusses how to write tests for PHP effectively.

Process must be respected

Rather than enforcing something called **process** on the team members, it is a good idea to get the team to define, agree, follow, and improve the process themselves. It is a fact that the software we develop with PHP is no longer simple. If we try to make the software over simplified, the chances are that the users might find the software we develop useless, and the users will loose the purpose of employing a team to develop the software. Therefore, the better approach is to understand the true complex nature of today's enterprise software and be prepared to deal with complexity.

Trying to be quick and overlooking details is short lived. A very heavy process where team members spend more time on non-real work also kills. The best is to have a process in place that the team is comfortable living with.

The element of the people factor in a process is critical to the success of the PHP project. The process is a set of activities, and the team members need to practice those activities. Defining a process is the easier part, but getting the team to follow that is the most important, and sometimes most difficult.

If we refer to any book on software engineering, we can find loads of information on various software process models. However, most of those traditional processes would not be a good fit for a PHP project. We might not need such rigor that is demanded by traditional software processes in a PHP project. Also, the dynamic and energetic nature of PHP developers would not tolerate a rigorous process, making it hard to get them to follow and adhere the process.

If we are to use our own, self-made process for our PHP team project, we still can borrow from the traditional process models. We should pay attention to the following key areas in a software process:

- Understanding user requirements
    - What do the users want?
    - How can we model exactly what is in users' minds?

- From model to design
    - What should be the right design (both, architectural and user interface) that would help realize the model that matches user expectations?

- From design to implementation
    - Get the design and convert that to a working implementation

- Test
    - Verify that implementation matches users' expectations
    - Find gaps between what the users wanted and what the developers really implemented

- Fix
    - If there happens to be gaps between what is expected versus what was implemented, then fix those issues

- Verify
    - Verify that the system works after fixing any bugs

- Feedback
  - ○ Deliver to the user and collect user feedback
  - ○ Be prepared for changes
  - ○ If changes are required, start a new cycle with requirements gathering and follow through the process cycle again

Software teams prefer short iterative cycles, so that the user feedback can be facilitated sooner into the product, before the software has deviated too much from what the users really want. If we were to drift too much from user expectations, the effort required to rectify the direction would be too much.

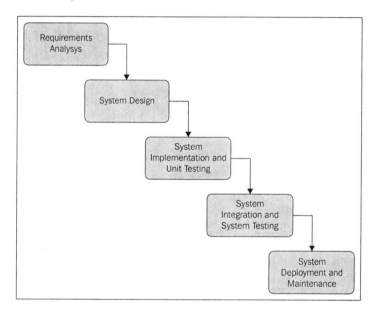

In a typical software process life cycle (as shown in the preceding screenshot), we start from the requirements analysis to understand the user requirements. Then, based on the requirements gathered, we do a systems design. Based on the system design, we do the system implementation. The implementation is done by multiple developers who are responsible for unit testing their own areas. Then, you integrate all of the pieces together and do system testing, to ensure that the entire system operates, as expected. Once the system tests are satisfactory, we can deploy the application to the live system, and the system maintenance begins. Rather than following these steps only once for a project, we can carry out several iterations of these steps to come up with the complete system.

Team members who are used to ad hoc development often tend to overlook the need for testing time, and more importantly, fixing and verifying time. While it can be assured that the developers might do a good job with the code for common cases, the value of testing comes when it comes to testing for edge cases. Sometimes, if these edge cases are not covered, the system might even come down to its knees, at the hands of a malicious user or even an ignorant innocent user. Therefore, it is a must to account for the time for testing, fixing, and verifying of issues; even with a PHP project. When we come up with time estimates, we must include some buffer time for these activities.

The software team can get together and design a process that suites them to cover these aspects of a process. That way, the team will be better off in understanding why each step of the process is in place. However, it is also important that someone in the team has good experience about past projects, so that he or she can ensure that vital parts of the process phases are not taken lightly or overlooked.

The alternative to defining our own process is to take a well-known process model and fine-tune it to meet our needs. This is a more recommended approach when choosing a process, as defining our own process from scratch is almost equivalent to reinventing the wheel. However, the challenge here is to get the team to follow the process. Because unlike in the case where the team invents their own process, the chances of the team members understanding each activity in the process is low.

 Follow the process. The most important aspect of a process is not the fact that a process exists, but rather the fact that the team members follow the activities defined by the process.

There are some characters that have fewer problems conforming with the process, as their goal is **quality**. There are others, who would rather focus on getting things done in a quick time. They will do their best not to follow the process, even if they understand its meaning, because they just feel hindered by the process in place. Teams always will and should include both kinds of persons to get the best out of both, as the group can help achieve quality and the other help reaching the goals in the given time.

From no process to some process

If there is no process at all used for the current project, it might seem as if it is impossible to introduce a process. However, moving from no process to some process is not very difficult.

If we are stuck in the vicious cycle of code-test-code, it is quite easy to convince the team about the benefits of a process. Just start tracking the number of bugs popping up each day, along with some rough estimates of the time spent on debugging (to locate the cause of the bug). It will be evident to anyone in the team, with some data, to figure out that the effort is wasted on debugging issues over and over again. Everyone will be delighted to find ways in which these wasted debug cycles could be saved.

 Bugs are inevitable in software. However, it is also possible to drastically cut down the number of bugs we generate, by being a bit organized.

The first step would be to analyze the kind of bugs that we have been seeing and understand the cause for them arising. Was it ignorance, lack of understanding on requirements, problems in interfacing the layers, and so on that were the root of the problem? And based on that analysis, we can figure out what can be done to improve in terms of quality, reducing the number of bugs.

For example, imagine that most of the bugs are in the user interface layer. Then, assuming that we are using a PHP framework, we can be assured to some extent that the bugs are not due to inter layer interfacing, because the framework is supposed to protect us with that aspect. Therefore, it might be a good idea to evaluate our presentation layer implementation techniques. If the team members who are involved with the presentation layer are experienced ones, we can be assured that the bugs are not due to the incorrect use of PHP programming constructs. If the team members are novice programmers, one of the first things that could be done is to review the code on a regular basis. For example, as soon as a module, or part of it, is completed, a code review can be held and the problems pointed out. If the programmers are experienced, the problems might be in consistency with respect to each other's work. If that is the case, the starting point would be to define some guidelines that should be looked into and followed during the implementation process. And for each report and form, when completed, there can be a brief review, with everyone in the room, just to ensure that the team is on track. These reviews would be required for only a few numbers of implementations to start with. After some time, everyone will be familiar with what will be done and the inconsistency problems would be gone.

 It is important to have **everyone in the team participate in the reviews,** be that a code review, design review, or just a brief review to verify some guidelines. Those review sessions become educational sessions, and let everyone learn from each other.

If we find that the user interface bugs are due to the lack of understanding about the user requirements, we can introduce a storyboard modeling session that everyone on the team can participate, prior to designing and implementing user interfaces. Note that it is not only the UI engineers, but also the others, such as those working on data layer and business layer team members, who should participate in these UI modeling sessions. This way, we can leverage the knowledge of those team members who have a better understanding on data and business aspects of the application in the UI. That will ensure we do the right thing and have all user-required elements in our user interface.

 User interface is the face of the application. It is the layer that the users get to see. It is common in most software applications that the **majority of the bugs reported would be against the user interface**.

These are some examples of how we can go from no process to some process that we discussed in the previous paragraphs. As you can see, going from no process to some process is not that complicated. Although it was only the user interface, in other words, the presentation layer, that we took as an example here, the same approach can be extended to overcome problems in the business logic layer and the data layer.

It is a myth that software professionals sometimes believe that implementing a process where there is none will be hard. Not only that it can be done, but also it can be done effectively, without facing problems such as team resistance. All that is required is to let the team understand how it can help to be effective and productive in saving their time and effort. Once the team gets used to it, they will see the value of it and would never want to go back to the vicious cycle of code and debug, ever again.

Process helps not hinder

A process can be seen as a burden if the people feel like they need to follow rules and obey them. That kind of feeling is very difficult to live with, when it comes to PHP developers.

As it was discussed in the previous section, it is not that hard to implement a process and get a team of PHP developers to follow it. The key to success is to pick and choose what fits our needs and use them.

Often, young developers want to occupy themselves with what they want to do. They want to explore new things, learn new things, and try them in practice. If they do not try new things, they will end up doing routine boring things, day in and day out. That would result in low productivity, and we would have a hard time getting things done on time. This is why we should get support from the project team to stick to the process in place. The team should be challenged to improve the process. They should be challenged to seek new ideas on how to develop the application so that there will be fewer bugs in the system against their names next time around. Therefore, the process can help ignite passion in the PHP developers to do the right thing when it comes to implementing the application. The team should view the set of activities defined by the process as helpers.

Simple process for PHP projects

In this section, we will look into a process model that we can use as a starting point for the PHP projects that we are working on. The process is designed with the MVC framework based design model in mind, which we have discussed in the previous chapter. It is assumed that the workload is broken down based on the Model-View-Controller pattern, and team members are assigned to work on each layer based on that breakdown.

The process model clearly depicts how the separate concerns such as the data layer, the business layer, and the presentation layer can be worked on in parallel, and at the same time, how those separate concerns fit with each other to form the entire system. If you carefully evaluate this process model, there is no activity for system integration. So one might question how the separate layers would be integrated with each other. However, if you pay attention to the design and implementation details of each layer, you will notice the dependencies mentioned in each layer, which lead to the integration. For example, business logic implementation requires the concrete database design, as well as the data access layer. The final user interface implementation would be done on top of the business logic implementation. Therefore, the integration of these independent layers happens seamlessly, along the way, in the process. If the team follows the process as it is, the integration would result in naturally.

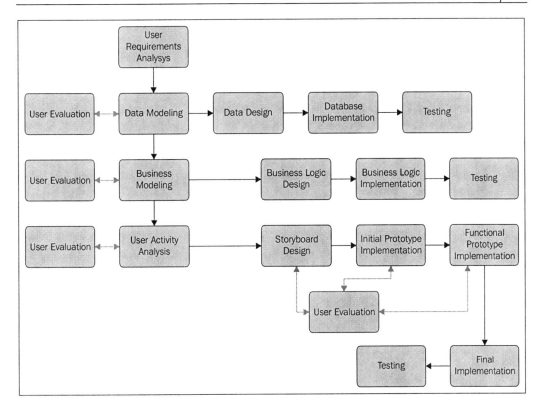

User requirements

The initial activity of the process model is to analyze the user requirements. It is obvious that in any software project, the first and foremost activity is to have an understanding of what the users require.

There are various tools and techniques to analyze user requirements. However, it is important to note that, while it is important to understand the user requirement in full, the idea here is not to write loads of documents, especially when it comes to PHP projects. What is more important is to make sure that we model what the users require and, based on the models, get the users to provide feedback, and then improve the model based on the user feedback. Some simple techniques that can be used to capture requirements include:

- Studying the existing system
- Observation of the users in action in a real environment
- Interviews with potential users and stakeholders of the system

Some tools that can be used to capture requirements include:

- Data flow diagrams showing how data flows and processing happens in the system

- Use case diagrams that portray how potential users of the system would be using the system. When using use case diagrams, it is critical to capture all of the major use cases of the system at a high level. It does not need to be too detailed, but we need to ensure that we have not missed any key use case scenario in the implementation. We can always seek the help of the users to help us validate the use cases and fill in the gaps, in case we have missed any key user requirements.

When documenting user requirements, we need to be comprehensive, concise, and clear. This is because the team members need to be able to refer to those, whenever they want. If the requirement specifications are too bulky and take time to read, it might not help the team. Therefore, it is always a good idea to use diagrams and tables to summarize information, whenever possible, to make sure that the captured information can be grasped by the team members at a glance.

We need to make sure that the team members really refer to the requirements to during the project life cycle. Therefore, anything that encourages them to use those requirement specifications is welcome and would make the project's success more probable.

Modeling what the users want

The purpose of the requirements gathering activity is to help us understand what the users want. The next step is to come up with a model that bridges the gap between the real world and the software world. For example, we need to be able to map the user requirements to the data model, and the business logic model, that we can implement with the software technology that we know.

Data modeling

Data modeling activities are supposed to produce the data model that represents the data involved with the system under consideration. Entity relationship diagrams are the most well known tool to help model data in a system.

Note that modeling data is the first activity following the user requirement gathering. This depicts the importance of the data modeling activity with respect to the design and implementation of the rest of the system. Most of the systems are all about effective data storage processing and presenting.

The outcome of the data modeling activity is a set of diagrams that represent the entities within the system and their relationship to each other:

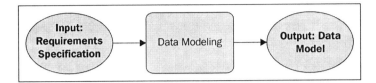

It is important to note that a data model is not the same as a database design. The model is the reference that can be used as the input to the database design activity, and the data model is also the input for the business modeling activity of the process. Data design will be explained later in this chapter.

Business modeling

Once we understand the data involved with the system, the next step is to understand the business activities carried out with those data. Business logic modeling can be done with tools such as data flow diagrams or use case diagrams. The objective is to understand what sort of business activities the users carry out with the software system being developed. The inputs and outputs of the business logic processing and the various data stores, where the data is pulled from, are modeled in this phase of the process. Like in the case of data modeling, we can validate the business model with the user and incorporate user feedback back into the model. It is also noteworthy that the business modeling activity is different from the business logic design activity. Business logic design is based on the business model that we develop in this phase of the process.

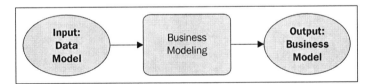

The output of the business modeling activity is the business model. Simply speaking, it is a set of diagrams that represent the use cases or the data flow. Like in the case of data model, the business model should also be simple to refer back, if team members require to do so.

Once we have both the data model and the business model, we can move on to the user activity analysis.

User activity analysis

While executing business functions with the software application, users engage in various activities using the system. Analyzing those activities becomes the next important activity in the process, and it also opens up the doors to understanding and designing the user interface.

Based on the business model and the data model, we can analyze the various activities that the users would want to carry out with the system. We can make use of the data processing functions of data flow diagrams, or use case diagrams, and come up with a list of user activities for each business use case of the system.

The list of user activities becomes the input for the storyboard design activity.

Before looking into the details of the presentation layer design, let us step back for a moment and look into data layer design.

Designs and implementing the data layer

As mentioned earlier, the process model proposed in this chapter is intended to be used for PHP projects, and therefore, is based on the MVC pattern. The data layer represents the model in MVC. In the design of the PHP application, we need to first attend the data layer.

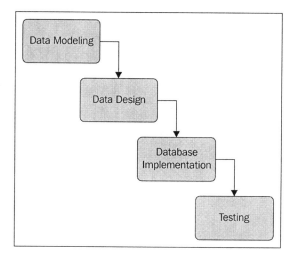

Using the data model as the input, we can perform data design. The data design can be independent from a specific database management system. However, the information, such as data types, needs to be taken into account. The number of tables, their relationships, the volume of data involved, and related performance implications need to be taken into account.

The next activity is the implementation, keeping open the option of switching the database management systems or supporting multiple database management systems open. In this activity, we might either use the database management systems directly or use SQL and try to be database agnostic. In addition to creating the database, the team members involved with the data layer implementation also devise plans for testing and also for carrying out unit testing.

In addition to SQL based unit testing, they need to implement the database access logic, which is also a part of the database layer, using PHP. The team members can then implement unit tests with PHP to verify the implementation. Executing the unit tests can be automated using PHP frameworks, upon each source code change.

Once the implementation is complete, it can be tested and verified completely using system testing by a quality assurance team.

Database implementation is a prerequisite for business logic implementation. However, business logic design need not wait until the database implementation is complete. As soon as data model is available, business modeling can be done and followed by business logic design. It is the business logic implementation that requires database implementation. The business layer sub-team can start its design work in parallel with the data layer sub-team and work side by side on their designs.

Designs and implementing the business layer

Output from the business modeling activity is the input for the business logic design activity. The main objective is to design algorithms required to implement the kind of business logic that the users want the system to execute. We can use a natural language, as well as sequence diagrams, as tools in this phase. As PHP is close to natural language, we can use PHP in place of natural language for the business logic design. However, the risk here is that it can degenerate into coding activity. Therefore, it is advisable to use sequence diagrams and natural language, as per requirement, and only use PHP when it comes to the real implementation.

Business logic implementation is to implement the designed algorithms with PHP. We need to have the database access layer available for this phase. Unit testing can be done along the way to verify the implementation, the logic, algorithms, and the data processing. It is also welcome to automate the unit testing. This will verify the system to guard against regression when changes are done.

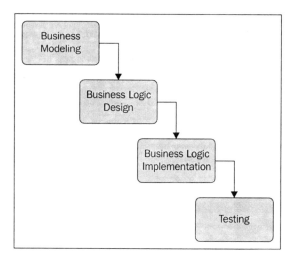

Implementation should carefully evaluate the need for the design and implementation of APIs. Also, the use of object-oriented features versus functional features of PHP should be evaluated. PHP code reuse, proper use of the PHP framework in place, as well as adhering to defined coding guidelines and best practices, must be given due attention in this phase of the process.

Once the implementation is done, system testing can be done to verify the implementation against the requirements. Note that we can start testing as soon as an independent module or a sub-system reaches completion in terms of implementation, without waiting for the entire system to complete. This way, we can make sure that issues are found earlier, and the development team as well as the testing team are kept busy all of the time.

Design and implementation of the user interface

The output of the user activity analysis is the input to the user interface design phase of the process. Business modeling is followed by the user activity modeling. User interface design can take place in parallel with the data design and business logic design. However, for the implementation of the user interface layer, the business logic implementation must be available.

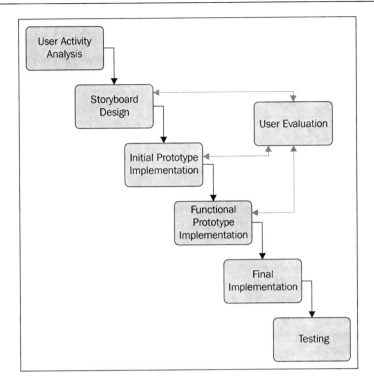

The first activity in the user interface design is the design of the storyboards. It is a rule of thumb that, for each user activity, there will be a corresponding user interface element in the user interface. Therefore, we should have a storyboard for each user activity that we have identified.

Storyboard design can be done on a white board or with a pen or pencil and paper, with some rough sketches, to capture and model the user interface elements to support the user to interact with the system. The best practices, human computer interaction guidelines, as well as the consistency guidelines, should be taken into account in this phase of the process. We can get the storyboard designs reviewed by the users. Once we get the user feedback, and incorporate the feedback to the design, we have some agreement between the users and the team on the design. Then, we can move on to the next activity in the process, the prototyping phase.

With prototypes, we can convert the storyboards into an initial working model of the application. We can use PHP and HTML to get the job done in this phase. We can even make use of the PHP framework that we are using for the PHP project to build the prototype.

When building prototypes, there can be two modes of operation. One is to build the prototype to be thrown away later, to start on the real implementation from scratch. The other mode is to implement the prototype, so that it can be used later for the real implementation. Both modes have their own pros and cons. The throw away model reveals us the shortcomings in the design to us and helps us to fix those and come up with a better design later on. However, throw away models waste time, as we are working on something to be thrown away and that would not contribute to the final product. Prototyping with the objective of using that for the final product saves time. But the problem with that model is that a weakness in design of the prototype, if any, would be also inherited by the final implementation. With PHP, we can be flexible, and willing to throw away any bad designs, and in case the prototype is deemed to be good, use the same as the base for the final product.

The initial prototype can only focus on the layouts, without bothering with functionality and connecting that to the model or controller in MVC. Once we show that to the users and get their feedback, we can move on to a more detailed functional prototype implementation. That detailed implementation needs to make use of the business logic implementation and the database. Again, the idea of this functional prototype is to capture user feedback, and we must use the PHP framework that we plan to use for the project for this. Also note that given the time and effort that we are going to spend on the functional prototype, it would not be a good idea to throw this away. Therefore, we need to take some effort to make this as close to the real implementation as possible. If there are problems, we should fix these as early as possible. The functional prototype also needs to be run by the users and their feedback should be noted down and incorporated. One of the problems with the functional prototypes being evaluated by the users is that, because they are functional, the users might tend to mistake those with the final product. Therefore, it must be clearly communicated to the users and noted down that it is a prototype for evaluation purposes and not the final product by any means.

Once both the developers as well as the users, are happy about the prototype, we can move on to the final implementation of the presentation layer. As in the case of the implementation of the other layers, the developers can take care of the unit testing in this phase. There are tools that can automate web-based interface testing that the developers can make use of in this phase.

As and when modules are completed, those can be tested by the QA team.

The user interface sub-team of the PHP project team, can work closely with the business layer and data layer sub-team to make sure the success of the overall project. After all, it is a single project as far as the users are concerned, and for the product being developed to be useful, each part has to work with each other seamlessly.

Summary

In this chapter, we discussed the need for a software process model for a PHP project. With a powerful yet simple programming language like PHP, the usual temptation is to overlook the need of a process. However, the increasing complexity of the PHP applications demand a systematic approach from start to end of PHP team projects nowadays.

Though it is seemingly difficult to define a process and get the team to follow that process, as it was discussed in this chapter, it is quite possible to implement a working process model and get the team to follow that. The secret of success is to get the team involved and let the team members themselves understand the need of a process. Start simple and improve as required and consciously evaluate where we are in terms of our process and identify where we want to go. A simple measure, such as the number of bugs, their frequency, and the nature of those, would reveal where we are in terms of the process. Reducing the number and frequency of the bugs would be the next immediate objective, based on which we can formulate a process to start with.

In this chapter, we also discussed in detail how following a process model can help improve the quality of the software that we develop. Guidelines and best practices can be used to improve the quality of the work done by team members. Regular reviews can further enhance the team's ability to produce quality software. And, as it is the users who really have the final say about the quality of a system, we are better off engaging with the users as much as possible, getting their feedback on what the project team produces on a regular basis, and incorporating their feedback to the system being developed.

In the final section of this chapter, a process model, which can be used for PHP projects, was introduced. This process model is designed with the use of the MVC design pattern in the PHP projects in mind.

This process model will be a very good starting point for your PHP projects. You should be able to improve it and customize it to suit your needs, when you gather more experience with the projects.

In the next chapter, we will discuss the agile principles, and how the concepts discussed in this chapter relate to the agile principles.

5
Agile Works Best

In the previous chapter, we discussed a process model that can be used for PHP projects. We can use the process model as the base for our projects and can also succeed with the projects that we are working on. If you have a second look at the process model that was suggested, you will note that the need for getting feedback from the users is highlighted in multiple places. This was done very consciously and with a purpose.

We are developing software for users, and we want to ensure that the software is really useful for the users. Over time, people working on this software have faced the same problem over and over again. Therefore, they have come up with a concept called **agile development**. In this chapter, we will explore the concepts of agile development and will also see how these can help us with the PHP projects.

In this chapter, we will cover the following:

- Introductions to agile philosophy, including agile values and agile principles
- Common problems and fears that developers face while developing a product
- What is meant by agility and how it can help
- Extreme programming principles
- Advantages of agile process models
- Team agility
- Agile process models
- Agile principles for the PHP project team

Introducing agile philosophy

Agile methodology consists of the following two parts:

1. Agile values

2. Agile principles

Agile values

Agile values identify the key characteristics of the way in which we develop software. These values attempt to avoid those practices and norms that tend to cause problems in the development of a software application.

> Manifesto for Agile Software Development:
>
> We are uncovering better ways of developing software by doing it and helping others do it.
>
> Through this work we have come to value:
>
> Individuals and interactions over processes and tools
>
> Working software over comprehensive documentation
>
> Customer collaboration over contract negotiation
>
> Responding to change over following a plan
>
> That is, while there is value in the items on the right, we value the items on the left more.
>
> Source: http://www.agilemanifesto.org/

These values try to address the key factors of success when it comes to developing quality software. The rationale is not to overlook the values on the righthand side, rather to focus more on the values on the left hand side. By having more of those values on the left, we become more agile, thus responding to changes quickly.

Agile principles

The agile principles help us to stay focused on agile values throughout the project's life cycle. These principles nurture agility in a project's team. The principles are as follows:

Principles behind the Agile Manifesto

We follow these principles:

Our highest priority is to satisfy the customer through early and continuous delivery of valuable software.

Welcome changing requirements, even late in development. Agile processes harness change for the customer's competitive advantage.

Deliver working software frequently, from a couple of weeks to a couple of months, with a preference to the shorter timescale.

Business people and developers must work together daily throughout the project.

Build projects around motivated individuals.

Give them the environment and support they need, and trust them to get the job done.

The most efficient and effective method of conveying information to and within a development team is face-to-face conversation.

Working software is the primary measure of progress.

Agile processes promote sustainable development.

The sponsors, developers, and users should be able to maintain a constant pace indefinitely.

Continuous attention to technical excellence and good design enhances agility.

Simplicity--the art of maximizing the amount of work not done--is essential.

The best architectures, requirements, and designs emerge from self-organizing teams.

At regular intervals, the team reflects on how to become more effective, then tunes and adjusts its behavior accordingly.

Source: `http://www.agilemanifesto.org/principles.html`

The following sections describe the agile values, as well as agile principles in detail:

Individuals and interactions

Agile philosophy values individuals and interactions over process and tools. In the process that was introduced in the previous chapter, the three main sub-teams working on the data, business logic, and presentation layers have their own activities to follow. Moreover, they have their own tools that they use. However, as it was mentioned, it is of paramount importance that each sub-team interacts with each other.

Not only that each sub-team should interact, but also, there should be a helping communication between the members within sub-teams. If the team members interact, it becomes so easy to solve problems, such as inconsistencies in the PHP code that is written and the user interfaces that are designed. Moreover, that will also enhance the reuse of the PHP functions, classes, and the written API methods. This is because through interactions, individual team members can educate each other on what the system has and what the system is about. They can also share their technical expertise. Programming can be done in pairs so that more than one pair of eyes would be looking at the code, as it is being written. However, interaction should not be restricted to only those individuals who work on the same code. Interaction should take place between all of the team members who work on the project. This is because no matter how large the software project or the product would be, they all work on building a single application. It needs to run as a single application at the end of the project.

When it comes to placing the members into sub-teams, it is useful to identify an individual's traits, preferences, and skills. Moreover, it is also useful for each individual in the team to get to know each other so that they can share and relate to know how, create better designs, and overcome problems by sharing experiences. After all, it is about that human touch among the members, and no process or tool can bring about that value into a team.

Working software over comprehensive documentation

We can spend weeks, if not months, documenting system requirements. Some call this **analysis paralysis**. You'll never get out of the system requirements analysis phase. However, what is most important is to get the software that we are developing to a working state. This is done so that the users can use it for real life tasks and get their jobs done.

Documentation is required for some aspects, especially when it comes to user documentation. However, that is also a part of the software. In the traditional software process, before any working piece of code was written, bundles of documents were written on what the requirements were and what the design should be like.

It is important to understand the user environments and have some reference points to refer to them if the need arises. Often, a set of diagrams alone can capture what is required, and we can move on to make the software functional.

Customer collaboration

In traditional software processes, there was this notion that the client would sign the requirement specifications before proceeding to the implementation phase. It is a fact of life that the real world changes. The requirement specifications that you signed today can expire tomorrow. Moreover, when the system is delivered, the client might see that the software doesn't fit their purpose. This will result in the system being discarded by the users and will be branded as low quality.

It is for this reason that there were so many user evaluation and feedback phases that were added to the process. That was introduced in the previous chapter.

When we closely collaborate with the clients, making them a part of the process, and giving them the opportunity to have their say early and often in the process, there are chances that we make the software that we develop fit the bill for their use.

It is often the case that the users will not know for themselves what they want. After all, if they knew, they would not have hired us to develop the software for them. They would have done it themselves. Therefore, it is our job to make them understand what they want, along the way, while we develop what they want. Moreover, you will note that the team will also be learning more and more about the system, as the project progresses. The best way to expand the understanding, both of the users and of the team, is to collaborate with customers very closely and on a regular basis.

Responding to change

Change is inevitable. Therefore, it is not feasible to stick to a plan and follow that. If we are to adopt a change, even the plan we should change over time.

A process model provides us with a framework that will guide us on what to do and when to do. It is a good plan to help us stay on the course. However, we need to understand the need for change on the part of the users. We cannot afford to not respond to the changes requested by users, simply because we are in the middle of our process (in other words, in the middle of our plans). It is for this reason that we should have ample room for incorporating users' feedback into what we are designing and developing. More often than not, feedback comes disguised, as the requests change. As the users do not know the internals of the software application, their wishes might be beyond the scope of developers. Nevertheless, these expressions from users will be an important feedback. The key to success is to make sure that all of the project's team, as well as the users, are comfortable with the changes.

Customizing agile to our needs

Every project is unique. Therefore, we can learn from agile values and customize them to suite our project's needs. The process model that was introduced at the end of the previous chapter is a good starting point. Moreover, we can follow that model with agile values in place. The process can be enhanced and complemented with agile values, and can be customized and fine tuned as the time goes by.

Common fears for developers

In this section, we will discuss some of the fears that developers face while working on a software project. We need to pay attention to these fears because they can impact the project's success. First, we need to understand what these fears are. Then, we need to understand their implications on the project's success. This understanding will help us to cope with them in the correct manner. We can also prevent them from getting in the way of the project's team members, when reaching towards project's success.

Producing the wrong product

The project will produce the wrong product if we do not clearly understand the requirements of the users. There's always the possibility of a gap between what we understand and develop, and what the users want. We can try and bridge this gap, which we will discuss later in this chapter. If we let this gap stay as it is, we will end up producing the wrong product. The developers will be negatively affected if the wrong product is produced. On the other hand, it is bad for the developers' reputation. Producing the wrong product will also affect the confidence level of the developers. If the product that was produced by the developers was the wrong product and got rejected by the users, it will have a long-term impact on the careers of all of the developers in the project's team.

Product of inferior quality

While producing the wrong product is the worst case scenario, producing a product with inferior quality also has a negative impact on all of the members of the project's team. A product delivered with inferior quality will reduce the confidence that the management team has on the project's team. This will also affect the moral of the team members. Therefore, everyone on the project's team fears delivering a low quality product.

Getting late to complete the project

Not all, but many projects run late. The project will be late due to various reasons. One of the things that can make the project late is misjudgment of the requirements and the misjudgment with respect to the technology chosen for the project. If we choose an incorrect technology, it will cause us to run into many technical problems while delivering the real work. The dangers of the delay with a project include losing the project. Because of this, the organization will lose revenue opportunities. It also affects the future business of the organization. It will also affect the team members individually because they will be deemed as not capable of completing the assigned tasks on time. That will have a negative impact on the image of the team members and the organization's leaders. A project that is getting delayed is often looked at, as a cost center in an organization, rather than the revenue-generating engagement. Therefore, during the next round of performance evaluation and salary reviews, the team members who were part of the project that was delivered late will not have many positive reviews. This will also affect their respective careers in the future.

It is important to note that when the specifications change, the resulting implementation times can also vary. Therefore, calculating time buffers for such unforeseen scenarios is important. In the following sections, we will discuss how agile development will help reduce delays or help us to identify the possible delays early in the project. This can be done by effectively collaborating with the users and incorporating users' feedback into the product that is being built early and often.

Too much work in too little time

If the team starts feeling that the project is getting late, then there are chances that they will need to work for more hours (per week). Overworking has many negative consequences in addition to the immediate problem of having to work in the nights and kill rest. On one hand, it reduces the quality of life leading into all sorts of problems (for example, family and relationships related problems). On the other hand, it opens the door to a bunch of problems that will have long lasting impacts on the individuals and organization, such as stress, getting bored with what team members do, and deterioration of the quality of work. These long-term consequences will have far-reaching ripple effects. Therefore, as much as possible, we need to try and prevent doing overwork.

 Overwork also results due to slip-by bugs. Rushing to fix one bug and overlooking the overall picture can result in a snowball effect with respect to bugs. Tools, techniques, and metrologies that prevent sloppy work will cut down a considerable amount of rework and save time.

Traits of agile team members

Developers always look to overcome the fears that were described in the preceding section. The best way to overcome those fears is to ensure that they develop certain traits. These traits should help them to overcome the problem-causing situations that become the root causes for the above fears. In the following section, we will discuss the traits that are desired from the team members that follow an agile process.

Competence

Any project needs competent team members. However, unlike the traditional software development approaches, the agile process is much more sensitive to the team member's competence. This is because we entrust each member to deliver working software at any given time, and everyone in the team is assumed to deliver with expected quality. The project assumes motivated individuals, and the team is built on trust.

Common focus

The focus is to deliver early and often. Working software must be delivered to the client at all times. To achieve this, the team should have a common focus. If the focus is not unified, we need to waste time and efforts on getting all of the team members to pay attention to where we are heading. Therefore, it is desirable to have all the members in a team to focus on common objectives.

Collaboration

Collaboration requires good communication skills. As mentioned earlier, it is not only about talking or writing on what one wants, but also about listening and understanding what others want. Good communicators are also good listeners.

Decision-making ability

Agile teams are based on everyone's ability to do the job. There cannot be situations where some of the members need to lean on others for making a decision. It is a different matter that others can help, but each member should be able to stand up on their own and make their own decisions. In other words, everyone should be a leader. There can be a designated leader to make various cross-cutting decisions, but everyone in the team owns an important aspect of the final product. Therefore, everyone should be able to decide what is good and what is bad for that part of the system on which they are working.

Fuzzy-problem solving ability

Most of the problems that we need to solve, while helping users in building applications to run their business, cannot be solved using a mathematical approach. The real-world business problems are fuzzy. **Fuzzy** means that it is very difficult to define the problem precisely. Moreover, because those problems are solved by the software that we develop, our PHP project team should be able to deal with those fuzzy problems. This is one of the challenging areas that developers face, as the programming language constructs are logical and hardly fuzzy. We need to get the team members to deal with those fuzzy aspects of the problems. It is a mindset and technique, more than a technology.

Mutual trust and respect

Each member in the team has his or her own responsibilities, and we depend on them to deliver on those. Mutual trust is critical when we are dealing with each other. We can always verify on what everyone delivers. However, we need to trust them to deliver, rather than trying to micromanage individuals by thinking that they will deliver.

Respect is also as important as trust. We need to respect each individual's ideas, their approach, and their personal formation. Respect is most important when it comes to interaction. Respect encourages alternative views and voices, which is the secret of success when it comes to technically-excellent designs. Every individual in the team should be respected so they become comfortable in being an active member in the team.

What is agility

Agility includes effective, that is, rapid and adaptive, response to change. This requires effective communication among all of the stakeholders. Stakeholders are those who are going to benefit from the project in some form or another. The key stakeholders of the project include the developers and the users. Leaders of the customer organization, as well as the leaders of the software development organizations, are also among the stakeholders.

Rather than keeping the customher away, drawing the customer into the team helps the team to be more effective. There can be various types of customers, some are annoying, and some who tend to forget what they once said. There are also those who will help steer the project in the right direction. The idea of drawing the customer into the team is not to let them micromanage the team. Rather, it is for them to help the team to understand the user requirements better. This needs to be explained to the customers up front, if they seem to hinder the project, rather than trying to help in it. After all, it is the team that consists of the technical experts, so the customer should understand this.

Organizing a team, in such a manner so that it is in control of the work performed, is also an important part of being able to adapt to change effectively. The team dynamics will help us to respond to changes in a short period of time without any major frictions.

Agile processes are based on three key assumptions. These assumptions are as follows:

- It is difficult to predict in advance, which requirements or customer priorities will change and which will not.
- For many types of software, design and construction activities are interweaved. We can use construction to prove the design.
- Analysis, design, and testing are not as predictable from the planning's perspective as we software developers like them to be.

To manage unpredictability, the agile process must be adapted incrementally by the project's team. Incremental adaptation requires customer's feedback. Based on the evaluation of delivered software, it increments or executes prototypes over short time periods. The length of the time periods should be selected based on the nature of the user requirements. It is ideal to restrict the length of a delivery to get incremented by two or three weeks.

Agility yields rapid, incremental delivery of software. This makes sure that the client will get to see the real up-and-running software in quick time.

Characteristics of an agile process

An agile process is driven by the customer's demand. In other words, the process that is delivered is based on the users' descriptions of what is required. What the project's team builds is based on the user-given scenarios.

The agile process also recognizes that plans are short lived. What is more important is to meet the users' requirements. Because the real world keeps on changing, plans have little meaning. Still, we cannot eliminate the need for planning. Constant planning will make sure that we will always be sensitive to where we're going, compared to where we are.

Developing software iteratively, with a greater emphasis on construction activities, is another characteristic of the agile process. Construction activities make sure that we have something working all of the time. Activities such as requirements gathering for system modeling are not construction activities. Those activities, even though they're useful, do not deliver something tangible to the users. On the other hand, activities such as design, design prototyping, implementation, unit testing, and system testing are activities that deliver useful working software to the users.

When our focus is on construction activities, it is a good practice that we deliver the software in multiple software increments. This gives us more time to incorporate user feedback, as we go deeper into implementing the product. This ensures that the team will deliver a high quality product at the end of the project's life cycle because the latter increments of software are based on clearly-understood requirements. This is as opposed to those, which would have been delivered with partially understood requirements in the earlier increments.

As we go deep into the project's life cycle, we can adopt the project's team as well as the designs and the PHP code that we implement as changes occur.

Principles of agility

Our highest priority is to satisfy the customer through early and continuous delivery of useful and valuable software. To meet this requirement, we need to be able to embrace changes. We welcome changing requirements, even late in development life cycle. Agile processes leverage changes for the customer's competitive advantage. In order to attain and sustain competitive advantage over the competitors, the customer needs to be able to change the software system that he or she uses for the business at the customer's will. If the software is too rigid, there is no way that we can accommodate agility in the software that we develop. Therefore, not only the process, but also the product, needs to be equipped with agile characteristics. In addition, the customer will need to have new features of the software within a short period of time. This is required to beat the competitors with state of the art software system that facilitate latest business trends.

Therefore, deliver the working software as soon as possible. A couple of weeks to a couple of months are always welcome. For example, the customer might want to improve the reports that are generated at the presentation layer based on the business data. Moreover, some of this business data will not have been captured in the data model in the initial design. Still, as the software development team, we need to be able to upgrade the design and implement the new set of reports using PHP in a very short period of time. We cannot afford to take months to improve the reports. Also, our process should be such that we will be able to accommodate this change and deliver it within a short period of time.

In order to make sure that we can understand these types of changes, we need to make the business people and the developers daily work together throughout the project. When these two parties work together, it becomes very easy for them to understand each other.

The team members are the most important resource in a software project. The motivation and attitude of these team members can be considered the most important aspect that will determine the success of the project. If we build the project around motivated individuals, give them the environment and support they need, trust them to get the job done, the project will be a definite success.

Obviously, the individual team members need to work with each other in order to make the project a success. The most efficient and effective method of conveying information to and within a development team is a face-to-face conversation. Even though various electronic forms of communication, such as instant messaging, emails, and forums makes effective communication possible, there is nothing comparable to face-to-face communication.

When it comes to evaluating progress, working software should be the primary measure of progress. We need to make sure that we clearly communicate this to all of the team members. They should always focus on making sure that the software they develop is in a working state at all times. It is not a bad idea to tie their performance reviews and evaluations based on how much effort they have put in. This is in order to make sure that whatever they deliver (software) is working all of the time.

An agile process promotes sustainable development. This means that people are not overworked, and they are not under stress in any condition. The sponsors, managers, developers, and users should be able to maintain a constant pace of development, testing, evaluation, and evolution, indefinitely.

The team should pay continuous attention to technical excellence. This is because good design enhances agility. Technical reviews with peers and non-technical reviews with users will allow corrective action to any deviations from the expected result. Aggressively seeking technical excellence will make sure that the team will be open minded and ready to adopt corrective action based on feedback.

With PHP, simplicity is paramount. Simplicity should be used as the art of maximizing the amount of work that is not done. In other words, it is essential that we prevent unwanted wasteful work, as well as rework, at all costs. PHP is a very good vehicle to achieve this.

The team members that we have should be smart and capable. If we can get those members to reflect on how to become more effective, at regular intervals, we can get the team to tune and adjust its behavior to enhance the process over time. The best architectures, requirements, and designs emerge from self-organizing teams. Therefore, for a high quality product, the formation of the team can have a direct impact.

Extreme Programming (XP)

Extreme Programming (XP) is the most widely used agile process. The characteristics of XP can be used very effectively for a PHP team's projects. It is a disciplined approach for software development that focuses on customer satisfaction. XP focuses on capturing user's requirements through simple tools. Releases are planned as a series of iterations. Tests are defined up front at the beginning of the project iterations. Smaller releases are done based on customer acceptance tests.

XP planning

XP planning begins with the creation of user stories that are used to capture requirements. Then, the team assesses each user story and assigns a cost based on estimated time and effort required to complete the user story. After that, user stories are grouped together for a deliverable increment and a commitment is made on the delivery date. After the first increment is completed, based on how the increment was accomplished, subsequent delivery dates for other increments would be defined.

XP design

The XP design follows the **KISS (keep it simple & smart)** principle. Simple design techniques, such as **CRC (Class, Repository, and Collaboration)** cards can be used to initiate the design. CRC cards are a brainstorming tool used to design the object-oriented software. They are used to write down the information on classes in the object-oriented system, and can help to keep the complexity of the design at a minimum. However, the final design should be in the code. Therefore, conscious effort is made to use the code for design. PHP is ideal for this purpose. For difficult design problems, prototypes could be developed with PHP, which can be depicted as spike solutions to help better understand the user problems and come up with better design solutions.

One of the challenges of going into the PHP code for design is that the initial code that we write will lead to problems with respect to the ideal design and implementation. The solution is to encourage refactoring the PHP code. The iterative refinement of the internal program design will lead to perfection of the design over time.

XP coding

In the XP approach, it is recommended to construct unit tests before the coding commences. This ensures that we can test as soon as the code is available. The other key advantage is that by looking into unit testing before the real implementation, we can make sure that we cover all the edge cases in the implementation, thereby leaving little room for bugs. This model also enforces simplicity because instead of worrying about making the code overly complex, the tests are written first and then the minimal code is written to cover only those test cases.

The concept of pair programming is one of the most popular aspects that XP is well known for. Based on the concept of 'two minds are better than one', a pair of programmers, rather than one, will work on a single piece of code. One will look over the shoulder of the other while the other one attends the code. This practice, as you might know by experience, ensures that we make the code better on the spot. Over time, due to the number of bugs being eliminated, thanks to this practice, the employment of two resources to write one module pays off.

The approach for choosing pairs is again up to the team. For PHP projects, we can get members from the same sub-team to pair up or members from different sub-teams to pair up. For example, two people form the presentation layer could work on a presentation aspect. Alternatively, one from the business layer can pair up with one from the presentation layer. If different sub-team members are paired up, it will ease integration pains in the PHP project, and the cross-domain know-how will also enhance among the team. As we saw at the end of the previous chapter, business layer implementation needs to wait until the data layer is available, and the presentation layer needs to wait for the business layer. This opens up the opportunity for pairing across the sub-teams so that presentation layer team will not need to wait idle until the people in business layer complete their task. We can use the idle time for the betterment of the overall project by means of paring up.

XP testing

The approach for testing in XP is based on 'test early and often'. All unit tests are executed daily. This will expose regression and shortcomings in the design.

Acceptance tests are defined by the customer and are executed to assess the customer-visible functionality. The project's team will help the users to define those tests. It is almost as if the customer will do system testing, which will convince the customer on system quality and its readiness to be deployed into production.

Advantages of agile development process

An agile development process can deliver successful systems quickly. Users will perceive the systems to be of high quality, and will make real use of those systems for the betterment of the business. Agile software engineering development guidelines stresses on on-time delivery of the operational software that will increment above generating analysis and design documents.

Agile development focuses on continuous communication and collaboration among developers and customers. This too contributes to quality. Agile software engineering embraces a philosophy that encourages customer satisfaction, and communication is the key to understand what they want. Incremental software delivery also contributes to user satisfaction because they get to see the system and evaluate if that is really what they want at the earliest, and provide feedback if that is not what they want.

Team agility

An agile team is able to respond to changes during project development. This is because agile development recognizes the need for the project's plans to be flexible. Changing something that one has developed over many weeks, if not months, is a pain. But changing something written in PHP is comparatively trouble free. For example, if you take a compiled programming language, such as Java or C, it takes considerable efforts to compile and run the system, before the changes are verified to not have any side effects. But with PHP, there is no compilation, therefore changing and testing is comparatively easier. Therefore, there is no need to panic at all about the need to change the implementation.

Attitudes of the individuals matter, both at the personal level and at the team level. All team members, irrespective of their personal traits, need to be willing to communicate with all others in the team. Not only communicating what you think and what you want, but also understanding what others want and think must be paid due attention. Effective communication includes effective listening and the willingness to open the minds to conflicting view points. To facilitate this, team structures and attitudes need to be nurtured and evolved. When it comes to communication, it should always be remembered that developers, as well as the customers, are a part of the same team. There is nothing to hide from the users because the system is for the users. This is where the open source style of development can help a great deal, where the developers discuss the design decisions on an open-mailing list and the stakeholders, such as users can voice their opinion openly. Everyone becomes a part of the system that is being developed.

The traditional thinking is that users use what developers develop, and that leads to the separation and division between customers and developers. Agile looks to eliminate this user and developer gap because the developers develop what the users want.

Note that we mentioned the need to deliver the software in incremental phases. However, it must be emphasized here that the rapid delivery of operational software is very important. The iterations are not intermediate work products. Rather, they are parts of the final system that the users can use in the real business environment. In other words, deliver the client-usable software, instead of functional prototypes, as soon as possible.

Agile process models

We have discussed Extreme Programming earlier, as it is the most widely used agile process. In the following sections, we will discuss some additional agile process models that are in use.

Adaptive Software Development

The philosophy driving **Adaptive Software Development (ASD)** is that self-organization arises when independent members in a team cooperate to create a solution to a problem that is beyond the capability of any individual member.

Adaptive cycle is mission-driven, component-based, iterative, time-boxed, risk driven, and change-tolerant. **Mission driven** means that the team defines the objectives to be achieved through the process, and take up the project as a mission that must be accomplished. The **system** is defined as a set of components. In the case of PHP projects, each layer can have one or more components. Each iteration of the project will be time-boxed, meaning that we will come up with a well-defined schedule. Moreover, each iteration will have a well-defined time frame within which that iteration will be delivered. Throughout the project's life cycle, the project's team will watch out for possible risks and keep open the doors for changes. Risks can be successfully dealt with and mitigated, thanks to the change-tolerant approach of the project's team. Risk-driven planning allows us to be adaptive in the future iteration cycles.

Collaboration in ASD requires teamwork from a jelled team. The preferred requirements-gathering approach is a joint application development. In other words, prototyping is used for requirements gathering and requirements verification.

This process model facilitates team learning throughout the project's life cycle. First, the components are implemented and tested, and then the focus groups provide feedback. **Focus groups** are those sets of users who are involved and interested in that particular set of components and features that they encapsulate. This allows both users and developers to learn. Users learn what they are going to get, and how the system would look and feel when implemented for real using PHP. Developers can learn from the users what they really wanted and what the development team actually delivered. The development team can learn from what they did right as well as from what they did wrong, with respect to meeting user requirements. The formal technical reviews, as well as analyzing the success or failure of process iteration life cycles, contribute to team learning. The next time around, either in the next iteration, or in the next project, the probability of the team doing much better is very high.

Dynamic Systems Development Method

Dynamic Systems Development Method (DSDM) provides a framework for building and maintaining systems, meet tight time constraints, using incremental prototyping in a controlled environment. The guiding principle used in this process is the **Pareto** principle. This states that 80% of a project can be delivered using 20% of the time and effort that is required to deliver the entire project.

Each increment only delivers enough functionality to move to the next increment. Time boxes are used to fix the time and resources to determine how much functionality will be delivered in each increment.

Dynamic Systems Development Method's life cycle

Let's have a look at the Dynamic Systems Development Method's life cycle:

1. **Feasibility study**: This phase establishes the requirements and constraints for the project.

2. **Business study**: The objective of this phase is to establish functional and information requirements that are needed to provide business value. In a PHP project, with MVC pattern, this phase will identify the data model and the business logic model.

3. **Functional model iteration**: Functional model iterations produce a set of incremental prototypes to demonstrate functionality to the customer. Those prototypes also set the platform for user feedback.

4. **Design and build iteration**: In this iteration, the prototypes are revisited to ensure that they provide business value for end users. This can happen in parallel with functional model iteration that is based on the user feedback.

5. **Implementation**: The outcome of this latest iteration can be placed in an operational environment because it produces the final product, evolving prototypes into the final product, incorporating user feedback, and filling in technical gaps.

Scrum

The Scrum process focuses on small working teams that are used to maximize communication and minimize overhead. The process is adaptable to both technical and business challenges to ensure that the best product is produced. The process yields frequent increments that can be inspected, adjusted, tested, documented, and built on.

People performing development work are partitioned into clean, low coupling segments. This ensures that each partition, or sub-team, can work on their part, independent of each other. We need to carefully partition the work for the sub-teams so that there is less overlapping. The MVC based partitioning that we discussed in the previous chapters is a good model to achieve this.

Testing and documentation is performed as the product is built as a part of the development work. This ensures that not only the code, but the tests and documents are also available. Thus ensuring that the product that is being developed is completely developed. Often, it is the case that code will be the first thing that the development team focuses, and at the end, it will only be the code that is available. At that time, if we try to develop tests and documents, the chances of missing elements are high, as even the team members who wrote the code might have forgotten what exactly they themselves did. Therefore, it is always a good idea to perform testing and documentation as we go along.

The other key characteristic of the Scrum process is the ability to declare that the product is done whenever required. Constant focus is on the working software and the division of work items into working subsets. All of the working partitions, when put together, form the working software.

Backlog

Scrum uses the concept of a backlog to maintain the prioritized list of requirements or features that provide business value to customer. The items are attended to, based on the priority. Items can be added at any time and their priorities can be changed based on the customer's demand.

Sprints

Sprint, in the context of Scrum, is the work units required to achieve one of the backlog items. These work units must fit into a predefined time box, meaning that the Sprint must be completed within a predefined time period. The backlog items that are affected due to a higher priority backlog items are frozen to make way for highest priority items in the list.

Scrum meetings

Scrum meetings are intended to check the health of the process and the product. These are daily meetings of 15 minutes to discuss the following:

- What was done since last meeting?
- What obstacles were encountered?
- What will be done by the next meeting?

Demos

Demos, in the context of the Scrum process, deliver a software increment to customer for evaluation. Based on the feedback given by the customer, backlog items and their priorities will be updated and the next Sprints will be scheduled.

Feature Driven Development

As in most of the other agile style process models, **Feature Driven Development** emphasizes collaboration among team members. The complexity of the project is handled by using feature-based decomposition of the problem, followed by the integration of software increments. The technical communication is done using verbal, graphical, and textual means. Software quality is assured by using incremental development, design and code inspections, metric collections, and use of patterns in all areas, such as analysis, design, and construction.

In FDD, we develop an overall model that contains a set of classes that depicts the business model of the application that is to be built.

Then, based on this model, a features list is built. Features are categorized and prioritized and then work is broken up into two week chunks.

The project planning is then done by feature. Features are assessed based on priority, effort, technical issues, and schedule dependencies.

Design is also done based on each feature. Classes relevant to a feature are chosen first, and then class and method logics are written. An owner is assigned to each class. That owner is responsible for maintaining the design document for his or her own work packages.

The build system is also based on each feature. The class owner translates the design into source code and performs unit testing, and the integration is performed by a team leader.

Agile Modeling

Agile Modeling (AM) is a practice-based methodology for effective modeling and documentation of software systems in a light-weight manner.

Modeling is based on a set of guiding principles. First, modeling will be done with a purpose. Multiple design models are used to capture different perspectives. Out of the multiple models, only models with a long-term value are retained.

It is important to note that the model content is more important than the model representation. In the modeling process, it is important to get to know the models and tools that we use to create the models.

In the requirements gathering and analysis modeling phases, we need to work collaboratively with the customer to find out what the customer wants to do with the system. To ensure this occurs, once the requirements model is built, collaborative analysis modeling continues with the customer.

Architectural modeling derives a preliminary architecture from the analysis model. An architectural model must be real for the user's environment. Also, it must be understandable by developers because they should ensure that key characteristics of the model are preserved while constructing the system.

Agile for the PHP team

Now that we have a good understanding on the agile principle, let us discuss how the PHP team can benefit from the application of agile principles.

Pair programming

Pair programming will help in improving team bonding, team interaction, and will help each team member to uplift their standard. We can use all of the principles of pair programming that we discussed under the heading *Extreme Programming (XP)*.

Body language is important, therefore, they should sit side by side so that both partners of the pair feel comfortable.

The PHP code should be written while conversing with each other. Rather than criticizing each other, the pair needs to collaborate. They need to discuss the strengths and weaknesses of the PHP constructs used, conventions and guidelines followed, and the libraries and APIs used. The pair should focus on the elegance, efficiency, performance, and readability of the PHP code that they produce.

There are two roles that must be performed in a pair. The first role is the one who is at the keyboard and the other role is the one who looks at the PHP code that is written by the keyboard owner. The one without the keyboard has more time to think, and therefore will generate more ideas than the one with the key board. Over time, to avoid friction, it will be a good idea to switch these two roles too, on a regular basis. This will allow both members to have ample time to think as well as to work, so they can equally contribute with their brilliant ideas to the work at hand.

It is a common question to ask if it is worthwhile to spend two people to do the work that can be done by one. Note that it is not really true to say that two people are doing the work of one person in pair programming. Coding is not the most important part of the project. It is writing the right PHP code that syncs up with the correct design that is most important. In pair programming, while one is writing PHP code, the other is thinking ahead, looking for potential problems and corner cases. This will reduce bugs, increase system quality, and increase system acceptance by the end users.

Sustainable working style

Team members should work with passion and energy on the project. To make sure that the team members continue to work energetically, they need to have a room to recharge themselves on a daily basis. If this is not done, the team will not be able to work on the project with the same level of energy at all times. They will tear up, thus hindering the project's success towards the end of the project's life cycle.

To sustain the team's energy, the team needs to re-energize themselves. They should go home on time, take a break, take some time off from work, and spend time with family and friends.

If any team member is sick, they should be encouraged to stay at home. It is not productive for someone to work when they are sick. Going to work while suffering from an illness increases the risk of making other people in the team sick.

While at work, when team members feel tired, they should take a break. When team members make more mistakes than progress, then it is a clear indication that the folks are tired, and they should take a break. It is a good idea to have some coffee or tea, have some chit-chat, watch some TV, or play a game. Yes, you should have facilities in the office to facilitate those activities. It is not a good idea to only have a book shelf with some PHP books in the recreation area. There should be some activities that the team can enjoy.

Information-driven workspace

All members of the team should be sensitive to the current status of the project. Wandering around the work area should provide ample information about what is going on with the project. There should be enough white boards to capture ideas around the workspace. Rather than worrying about the neatness and beauty of the drawn diagrams, it is more important to have the ideas captured then and there. Therefore, it is perfectly fine to hand-draw the design diagrams and charts. There should be no rush to computerize the stuff. We can always use digital cameras to capture the white boards and can transfer them as notes to the computer.

For a healthy project, everyone on the team should have free and ready access to the information. Rather than looking and trying to understand the design, team members should be able to sense the design and reinforce that within the workspace, as they do their day to day work.

Simple charts can help to feed information into the team, and can help to evaluate, and thereby reinforce, the health of the project.

Some simple charts that can help you to improve the process include the following:

- Amount of pairing, as percentages, where people were working in pairs versus where people were working alone. This chart can help us to evaluate if we really use pair programming.

- Paring combinations, showing who pared with whom over a period of time. These can help us to evaluate our effectiveness of paring.

- Tests per second, showing how many tests were executed over a day. Also, showing in how many tests we passed (versus failed). This helps us to gauge our coding quality.

- Tracking the time to fix the found issues and the number of issues opened versus number of issues resolved. Continuously tracking the number of outstanding issues. This will help us understand the efforts required to solve the problems along with our ability to solve the problems quickly.

Fixing the process

Things will go wrong. Mistakes will happen. We need to learn lessons from them and move on. To fix those problems and prevent them in the future, we need to understand those problems, and especially why they happened. Root-cause analysis helps us in understanding the problems and figuring out the way to fix them in the way we work so that things don't go wrong again.

Also, in root-cause analysis, collaboration can help us in dealing with fixing issues in the process. We can share our conclusions and reasoning with each other, and can get everyone's perspective to ensure that we reach the best possible decisions to fix the process.

Sitting together

To collaborate among the team members in an effective manner, it is a good idea to sit together. Sitting together facilitates rapid and accurate communication. This means everyone, including the experts in design, business, programming, and testing, sits together. In this way, you have more opportunity to communicate clearly with each other, you also have the opportunity to learn from each other.

Sitting together reduces time to solve the problems drastically. You just turn around and ask someone who knows the subject. It also encourages you to ask for help, and you can get help when you need the most because there is no need to postpone.

It is not a good idea to ask the team members to sit with each other, against their will. However at the same time, the setup and layout of the work area should encourage people to sit together. The free flow of communication will not be encouraged if the workspace was arranged in such a manner that people were confined to their personal cubicles. At least have some common working areas so that people can sit comfortably and work with the other people, as and when they want.

One of the arguments against sitting together would be the background noise. However, over a period of time, people will realize that the energy of the project's team is flowing across the room. Thus, they will get used to the new model of working in a shared workspace. On the other hand, if the need for privacy arises for some activities like, meetings or calls, meeting rooms could be used for those things.

Remember, it is important to ask more questions, rather than having the team members or pairs trying to guess the things for themselves.

Ubiquitous language

When we develop software for business domains, we need to be able to communicate what we do, what others want, what the system is all about, and so on, to non-programmers and programmers.

Often, we are good at explaining the technical aspects related to the software and to the use of programmer's jargon. We are also capable of understanding what others tell us on the software and on the use of programmer's jargon. However, the challenge is to explain the system and what we are doing for non-programmers, and remember that system users are non-programmers. The idea is not to eliminate the use of technical terms, but rather to make sure that others also understand what we are talking about. The language that we use to describe things should be as close as possible to the real world domain (where the software is to be used).

Ubiquitous language reduces the risk of miscommunication among team members as well as between the team and the users. And note that even the PHP code that we write should reflect this language. Therefore, the function names, class names, and the names of the variables that we use should reflect this. Also, the language that we use should be in sync with the jargon used in the data and business models that we developed.

Stand-up meetings

It is important to know what others are doing in the team on a regular basis. It is always a good practice to eliminate the need for assumptions with respect to the rest of the team. When someone is stuck, others will be able to help because others have already gotten over that hurdle. That way, we can save tons of time, rather reinventing the wheel.

Stand-up meetings are about people interaction and participation. It needs to feel open and free. Therefore, it is important to do that in an open area, rather than around a cramped area. The environment should set the feeling for energetic and comfortable discussion.

It is not required to wait for the stand-up meeting to start the day. However, it is useful to start the day with the stand-up meeting. Moreover, the meeting should be short and sweet. As short as thirty seconds of speaking time (per person) is recommended.

The points to discuss should be crisp and clear. What did each team member do yesterday, what each member will be doing today, and what are the hurdles, if there are any. Moreover, pairs should also be picked, based on past experiences that other members have, to overcome hurdles found on a given day.

Irrespective of the fact that there is benefit in having stand-up meetings, it should not be taken as an excuse for one not to raise problems. If a pair hits a road block in the middle of the day, they should not wait until the next morning's stand-up meeting to communicate about it to the rest of the team. Communicate issues as soon as the issues surface, irrespective of the fact that there will be a meeting the next morning. This is because others in the team might need to discard some work due to the issue, as they didn't know that earlier.

Demonstrate the iteration outcome

Until the product is run for real, we cannot be sure if it will run and solve the problems that we actually have in our hand.

We can conduct weekly iteration demos to ensure that we have a running product on a regular basis. This would cut down on integration pains by a great deal. It also makes the team honest. They will admit to the breaks and bugs in the code or weaknesses in the design. It is important that the team has an open mind regarding the issues in the product that they develop.

The team needs to be honest with the problems and with the way they handle those with the stakeholders. This will ensure that we build trust with stakeholders. If the stakeholders lose their trust in the team, then that will not help the project in the long run.

Weekly deployment of the product in the real deployment environment will help the team realize the real issues.

Summary

In this chapter, we discussed the concepts related to the agile development practices in detail. Agile practices help us to deliver software that will maximize business value of the systems that we develop for the customers.

Agile philosophy confronts many traditional software practices. This is done to ensure that we can deliver software that is working and reliable, in a faster and more effective manner.

Self-organizing the teams, where each member takes the initiative and responsibility to deliver, is recommended. The working software is at the heart of the agile processes. These teams need to collaborate among themselves, as well as with the system users, to ensure that the delivered software meets expectations. Short delivery cycles, regular increments, regular demos, and deployment of the software being developed are important traits of the agile processes.

We can use PHP effectively to capture the requirements in the initial phases. This can be done using PHP as an effective means of building prototypes to capture the users' feedback. PHP programmers can pair up to minimize the possibility of bugs, and to increase the design and code quality. Different perspectives brought in by the various team members and the users will ensure that we get the product right.

Several flavors of agile processes were discussed in this chapter. This was done to help you understand the various means of adopting agile concepts to the PHP project on which you are working. Rather than just playing by the rules, it is ideal to try and evolve the current process to suite the project needs in an evolutionary manner. A team will not be able to go agile over night. However, slow and steady adoption of agile principles can win the challenge.

6
Ways of Collaboration

In the previous two chapters, while discussing process models and agile principles, the importance of collaboration has been stressed. In this chapter, we will be exploring the meaning of collaboration among team members, and the concepts and tools related to collaboration and communication.

Communication among team members prevents assumptions and conflicting work that is needed for the project's success. When multiple people are working on the same module or related modules, we need to ensure that the dependencies and inter-related work are managed properly. Information dissemination is a key requirement and should be done in such a manner that prevents assumptions and ambiguity. The team should be capable of achieving synergy with respect to the final product.

Source code is the means for achieving the final product in software projects. Therefore, source control is a must. Collective code ownership helps a team to ensure efficiencies in the development process. However, if source code control is taken for granted in a shared source environment, it will eventually lead to chaos. When a team of people work on the source code, you need some level of discipline to make sure that the code remains stable. You also need the help of tools to maintain that discipline throughout the project's life cycle.

No matter how much we try, we will not be able to write a bug-free code. Developers are human beings, and all humans are fallible. The problem is not the existence of bugs, but rather the way we approach them and tackle them. Similar to source control, dealing with bugs needs discipline to ensure that we effectively tackle the problems that we find in the source code.

When the software product is first developed, we will be thinking of it as a single product. However, over time, new modules would get added and not everyone will use all of the available modules. In different deployments of the same product, there will be different configurations. Therefore, in our PHP project, we should take steps to ensure that we manage multiple configurations effectively so that we are better off improving, upgrading, and fixing a given configuration at a given time.

Nowadays, there is a multitude of tools around to help the PHP team of developers to collaborate effectively. This is either amongst themselves or with other stakeholders of the project, such as users. Success of the team will depend on the selection of the correct set of tools and the effective use of those tools.

In this chapter, we will be covering the following:

- Challenges faced while working with teams
- Implications of assumptions made by team members
- Ensuring seamless integration
- Source control
- Bug control
- Configuration management
- Tools for communication and collaboration

 It is not the tools that matter, but the way in which we use those tools that determines a project's success.

Team work is challenging

It is challenging to work with a team. Putting together some smart people in a room will not deliver the results that we wish. The team members need to work with each other and organize themselves together for the team to operate as a single unit.

When a number of people are working together in a team, there can be situations where some people will need to work on the same component. Especially with pair programming, not only the pairs switch, but the components can also switch. Sub-components, that is, the independent parts of the same component, will be assigned to different members in the team to ensure parallelism to shorten the iteration lifetime. Thus, collaboration is a must.

Team members make assumptions

When team members are working on the PHP code, they might happen to make their own assumptions about what others are doing and what others might do. These assumptions are made unconsciously and team members will not even think of them as assumptions at times. However, they might lead to project iteration delays and sometimes can even be the root cause of a project's failure.

Lack of communication is the breeding ground for assumptions. When team members do not communicate enough, others are forced to move ahead with what they think others might do. When multiple parties make such assumptions, the chances are that those might drastically deviate from reality and can lead to crisis situations. For example, some members could need to throw away what they have done because others have already done it. Or some work might need to be redone because the work done so far does not seem to integrate with what others have done. Yet, some simple communication on the fact that someone is working on an algorithm or an API, or the fact that an assumption is going to be made on something, or just making some noise on what one might be going to do with respect to a design, would enlighten others on what is going on. From the previous chapter, it is clear that the stand up meetings are intended to do this kind of communication. We can also use a mailing list or a forum to do the same.

When using PHP libraries and APIs, there are so many alternative ways of doing the same thing. Communication and collaboration can help us ensure that we use the best alternatives for the kind of software application that we are developing. The pair programming can make sure that people share know-how and best practices with respect to using PHP, and discuss the alternatives to reach to the optimum solution.

The informative workspace that lets anyone know what is going on with the project also helps with making sure incorrect assumptions are not made. When information is flowing around, there is no need and no room for assumptions.

When team members are working on, say PHP code that implements the user interface layer, they need to have a look at the data model or the business model. It should be easy to find where those are. Sometimes the models are there, but very few know how to locate them into the project, especially when the team is busy with PHP code. Sometimes the modeling was done on white boards and wiped out, assuming those are pictured in the minds of the people involved. But the reality is that people forget. Even worse, they may think that they remember, but they might have forgotten one small, but important detail. Thus, it is best to capture and store them in an easily accessible manner. An image of the white board would do. All in the team should be able to know how to access it when the need arises. There can be a central location, a one stop, where the team members visit. This can help them to locate the images they are looking for, which have the design models.

Making integration possible

It is the general feeling that integrating different modules developed by various team members is a technical issue. However, it is a technical issue as well as a collaboration issue. For example, say we discussed the PHP library for some functionality required by the project with a third party and we missed the point for discussing what version should be used. Two of the team members who need to use this library go ahead and use it for their part of the project. One team member uses an older version of the library that he had downloaded on his machine, not knowing that it is not the latest version, and the other one downloads the latest version and uses it. However, when it comes to the integration phase, the team realizes that two versions of the library have different APIs or bugs, and the two team members have used elements of the library that are not common to both the versions. Lots of time and energy is wasted, as not only some work needs to be discarded, but also, people's morale goes down. How can we have prevented these sorts of frustrating situations? Some simple form of communication could have saved a lot of time. Say, a simple email mentioning that I am going to use this version. In a more systematic model, people can see a shared document that mentions the versions of the third party PHP libraries that are to be used for the project.

The other key aspect to keep in mind is that other members of the team are also stakeholders of the PHP code that you are developing. Often, this is well understood when it comes to data and business layers. However, it is also true at the user interface layer. As the user interface layer is built on top of the other two layers in a PHP project, it is common thinking that the user interface needs to consume the other layer, but no communication is required. But top-down and bottom-up communication is going to benefit the project. Those who work on the business logic layer and data layer needs to understand the nature and format of the presentation layer, what the users expect, and what the users' needs are. It is a fact that user expectations are evaluated while coming up with the data model and business model. However, note that they are done too early in the project iterations. It is at the depth of the project that we really get to see the real needs of the user. Moreover, it is with the user interface that we realize the expectations of the users. Therefore, unless the design is perfect, there are chances that we need to fine tune the system design at this stage. Anyone who has a bit of experience with software knows that it is virtually impossible to make a design perfect. Therefore, communication in either direction will make the product perfect and ensure project's success.

It is hard to make a team work if the team does not move along flawlessly. If there are hidden feelings about technical differences, it is hard to look in the eyes and be open about what is being said. If there are hidden feelings, it is not easy to get the real information out from individuals. Therefore, if the team is having difficulties, it will be worthwhile to consider some team building activities to help cultivate understanding and bonding.

Sometimes, we as human beings can hold so much complex information in our mind. However, over time, we tend to forget. When making integration happen, we need to have all of the information easily within reach. It is worth taking some time to record some of the things that we have in our minds. This can be done for the benefit of others so that when it is needed the most, they can access the information and move on, rather than getting stuck. Documentation, as it is well known in the software field, is a great way to capture the information of interest on the software system. People often concentrate on user documentation, but it is also important to have some form of design documentation as well, at least in the form of comments in the source code itself.

Integration is tough work and people can be pressured at times. Frustrations creep in when things do not work as they were expected to. Therefore, it is important to have some patience on the part of every one. Moreover, it keeps the minds open so that misunderstandings are kept away. It is much more important to keep your cool, rather than worrying about getting things done, because losing the cool will not get anyone anywhere.

Source control

When a team of people work together on a single project, we need to be able to make each other's code available to each other. There are various reasons for sharing the source code.

One key reason to share the source code is to make sure that others see the changes and improvements done to the APIs. For example, if the business layer sub-team optimized the business logic layer API, they would want to let the user interface sub-team know about this as soon as possible. The most efficient way of doing this is to commit the new changes to the shared source code repository and let the interested parties know over the desk, or by using some communication tool, such as instant messaging or a phone call.

The other important aspect of having PHP code of the project in a shared repository is the ability to have a look at any part of the code by anyone, whenever they wish. Note that PHP code is the most reliable form of documentation of the project. Therefore, if anyone is interested in any aspect of the code, the PHP code should be available in a shared repository and not only on individual team members' machines.

There are many source control solutions out there—Subversion (http://www. subversion.tigris.org/) and CVS (http://www.nongnu.org/ cvs/) are the two most well known solutions in this space. Subversion is the most used source control system these days. It was invented as the successor for CVS to overcome some of the problems and difficulties faced by developers.

Though the detailed commands used by various source control solutions vary, the concepts are common. Developers can check out the source code from the repository into their machines. They can make changes locally, and then can check the changes back onto the repository. Developers can check the difference between their local copies and the source code repository. They can also maintain different versions of the same source code.

It is common to use the terms trunk, branch, and tag with a source repository. The trunk usually contains the latest, bleeding source code. That is the place where active development takes place for a release or iteration. When the work for that release or iteration is deemed to be complete, a branch can be created. Once the branch is created, up until the release, changes required for the release, such as bug fixes can go into the branch, instead of the trunk. The risk of this model is that programmers generally forgets to merge bug fixes with the trunk. Therefore, all of the fixes done on the release branch should be ported to the trunk. The reason for not using the trunk for a release is that there can be some team members that do active development on the trunk. Therefore, the chances of the trunk becoming unstable are high.

When the branch comes to a stable state and the team decides that the release can be done, the branch can be tagged. The tag will indicate at which point in time, and with what PHP code, the release was done. The reason for tagging is that it is possible that in the future a new release could be done using a branch. If multiple releases are done from the same branch, we will be fixing at least a few bugs in the branch before each release. The tags at the point of release will help the team to locate the exact PHP source that was used for a given release if they wanted to find that in the future. Tags are meant to be static, fix point snapshots that are created at a certain point in time. A snapshot is read-only, meaning that its state should never be changed, unlike branches that are subject to change with the bug fixes and customizations done on them. Consider the following screenshot:

Index of /

Files shown:	0
Directory revision:	42640 (of 42640)
Sticky Revision:	[ ] Set
Query:	Query revision history

File ▲	Rev.	Age
branches/	42636	2 hours
tags/	41819	12 days
trunk/	42640	79 minutes

The preceding screenshot shows how the **trunk, branches**, and **tags** are organized in a Subversion source repository.

There are command line tools and graphical tools that can be used to deal with various source control systems. Based on the developer preferences, they can choose whatever tools they wish to.

To improve the overall team productivity, it is a good practice to recommend some common set of tools that the entire team uses. This will cut down the complexities when they try to fix problems with respect to the source repository. It will also be a good idea to have consensus on the features of the source control system that are to be used within the team.

If more than one person changes the same source, there are chances that when they commit the changes to the repository, the code could have conflicts. Source code control systems are capable of pointing out the conflicts and will force developers to resolve them. In order to resolve their conflict, they might need to sit together to figure out the root causes of the problem. It will help if they use the same tools to work with the common repository and figure out the conflicts by discussing the changes each person has done against the original code that they started with.

When we work on a particular branch and fix bugs in there, we might want to merge those with the trunk so that those bugs do not reappear in the future. The harder way of doing it is to commit the changes manually to both, the branch and trunk. However, most source control systems support the merge command that help you to merge the changes done on one location to another having the same source code.

It should also be noted that source control is often integrated with the IDEs. People can have their own preference regarding the IDE they use. However, it will help them all to have source control integrated to the IDE to improve their productivity.

When working with a team where the PHP code is shared using a commonly shared code repository, it will always be advisable to commit the changes done to the source code, then and there, to the common source code repository. Keeping the changes in an individual's local machine for too long will result in too many source conflicts by the time the individual checks them. That will also result in wide system breaks. The best practice is to commit all of the changes and improvements, as well as all new code, early and often to the common source repository. However, a good advice is to commit conceptual blocks of code, rather than in unrelated pieces. Never make a single commit that touches multiple modules or unrelated files, as we should be able to browse the commits as distinct entities. Also, never commit code that might have test failures or is not working. All developers must ensure that all code in the source code repository works for all team members all of the time.

Avoiding big bang changes on the PHP code is a very important principle. We should minimize surprises to other developers at all costs. Apart from causing surprises to the others, big bang changes also lead to bad design and quality problems. When something is written with PHP, it is good practice to develop it to some working state and commit that into the common repository without trying to make it perfect at the first effort. This will allow others to have a peak into the new source. Also, those who want to use it can give it a try and provide some feedback.

Note that, like emails, forums, and documents, PHP source code is a strong means of communication. In fact, PHP code is the best form of communication, as it is the most reliable form of documentation. When we develop an API, we are opening up a channel for others to use our logic. Therefore, the API needs to be self-descriptive and should have some API documentation in the source code itself. Moreover, when you use a common PHP code repository for the entire team, the power of source code, as a means of communication grows stronger. We can configure the source control system to send email alerts on the code changes that are committed by the developers to a mailing list. All team members can review it. This facilitates making the code the real basis of team reviews and discussions on the solution.

Bug control

As in the case of source control, the PHP project's team must use a bug tracking system (some also call it an issue tracking system) to keep track of bugs. As in the case of a source code repository, the bug tracking system will help the PHP project's team to achieve synergy around their activities, and around the bug tracking system.

There are various reasons to use a bug tracking system for the PHP project. First, we need to keep track of all of the issues because we tend to forget and miss the issues that we found. It is a common practice to leave a to-do note in the code itself. However, tracking these in a bug tracking system, rather than as to-do notes in the source code has many advantages. For example, we can generate reports on the issues and sometimes even do project management using bug tracking systems.

The following screeenshot shows an example report generated with an issue tracking system that shows the types of issues being raised in the system:

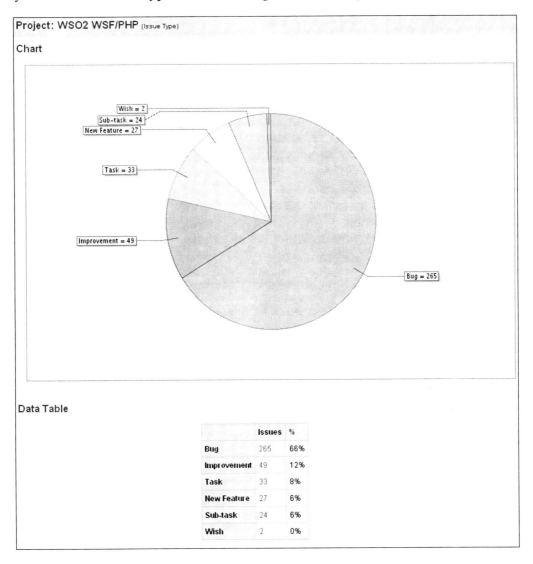

When the developers complete an iteration or a task, they move on to work on the next activities while the quality assurance team will start testing. The quality assurance team can use the bug tracking system to record issues, until such time that a developer would have some time to look into the issues. If the issue is critical (a show-stopper), we can get the developers to attend to that right away. However, if the issues are not showstoppers, the team of developers can choose to fix them based on the priorities of the activities on which they are working now.

The other reason we need a bug tracking system for the PHP project is to make sure that we can balance out the work load and spread out the team effort when attending the issues. For example, when a developer has completed the work that has been assigned to him, he can have a look into the open issues in the bug tracking system. The developer can assign the issue to himself to indicate that he is working on it and that others should not spend time on the same.

The bug tracking system can serve as another great platform for developers to collaborate. Usually, all bug tracking software systems have the facility to add comments. The developers, testers, and users can collaborate with each other through the bug tracking system. This is done so that they can educate each other on the nature of the issue and on the potential solution. When resolving an issue, the most important aspect is to be able to reproduce the issue. Developers can use the comments to record information that will help them to reproduce the problem. They can also provide potential fixes that might lead to the solution, and discuss pros and cons of the proposed solution. However, in a PHP project, rather than using the bug tracking system to discuss solutions, it would be far more effective to fix the code in pairs, right away. However, you will still need to record the bug for future reference.

Each issue in the system will have an associated status, priority, and severity.

The status indicates the current progress with respect to an issue. If the issue is **Open**, it means it is available for someone to be picked up and solved. **In-Progress** status means that someone is working on the issue, so no one else should worry about picking it up. The **Resolved** status means that someone provided a solution to the issue. **Closed** means someone verified the solution and the issue is no more. The set of states forms the life cycle of an issue. The following figure shows the life cycle of an issue in the issue tracking system:

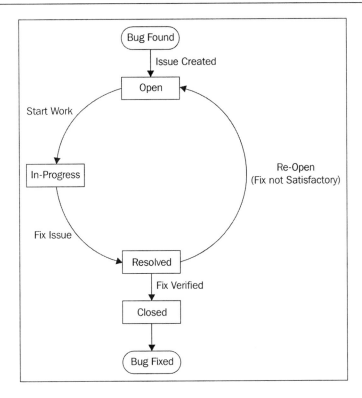

As the previous figure portrays, when a bug is found, an issue is created in the issue tracking system, and the issue will be in **Open** state. Once a developer starts working on the issue, the issue will transit to **In-progress** state. When the developer provides a fix, the issue is resolved. Then, the fix needs to be verified. If the verification fails, the issue will be re-opened and will go back to the **Open** state. If the verification is passed, the issue can be **Closed**, which indicates that the bug is fixed.

Priority indicates how soon the issue needs to be attended to. High priority issues are to be attended before the others.

Severity indicates the gravity of the issue. In other words, severity indicates the impact of the issue on the system.

Note that, often the difference between the priority and severity of an issue is confused. **Priority** means how soon the issue needs to be fixed. **Severity** means how serious the issue is. One may argue that high severity issues must be given high priority. That is not the case always. For example, we might have decided not to ship a particular feature for the next iteration. Therefore, the issues related to that feature, irrespective of how severe they are, need not be attended in this iteration. Therefore, those issues are not high-priority issues.

There are various reasons for bugs to appear in PHP code. The two main reasons are as follows:

- New code did not properly consider all use cases
- Changing the working code to fix one issue will break another

For both of these, as well as the other cases that cause bugs to appear in PHP code that we write, testing is the best way to deal with them. Testing can be carried out after the PHP code is written, but we need to think about how we are going to test before the code is written. That will force us to ensure that the design and the PHP code is bug free. To guard against regression, testing helps a great deal. Before one can finalize the implementation, he or she can run all of the tests available to ensure that there are no side effects due to the changes done in the code. If we do not have tests to run, this cannot be achieved.

One way to build a comprehensive set of tests is to write a test for each bug that appears in the issue tracking system. Each team member who fixes a bug needs to be encouraged to write a test case that verifies the fix provided. In the long run, we can use these tests to guard against regression issues.

Over time, the bug tracking system can turn out to contain a great wealth of knowledge to reflect the success of our process. From the data in the bug tracking system, we can get to know which layer of our PHP application had the most bugs. For example, is it the business layer or the presentation layer that troubled us the most? This data can lead us to the insights, as to what can be done to optimize the process.

Usually, it is the presentation layer that will have most of the issues in a system. It is because that is what the users see. Even though users may have reported the issue against the presentation layer, the real issue might be in the data layer or the business layer. Therefore, we need to have some mechanism to classify the issues raised.

Some issues are not really bugs, but are user errors, and might be solved with better documentation or better designed user interfaces. Some others are seen as bugs, but are really new features or improvements. Therefore, only a subset of the issues in the bug tracking system will be real bugs. The classification of issues will help us to deal with the real issues without complicating the matters. A very simple classification will include the following three categories of issues:

- Use error
- New feature or improvement
- Real bug

The issue tracking system can help us to analyze trends in development, testing, and the use of the PHP system that we have developed. Having fewer issues for a particular feature does not indicate that it is bug free. Maybe what that really means is that people are not using it, or **Quality Assurance** team is not testing it properly. Also, having many bugs on a feature does not mean that it is too buggy. Rather, it may mean that users are using it more and testers are testing it more.

Trend tracking can also help us to find the productivity, effectiveness, and workload of the team. For example, we can analyze the following:

- How many issues are assigned to a developer at a given time?
- How many issues were open versus how many issues were closed on a weekly basis?
- How many issues does a developer fix on a weekly basis?
- How much time, on average, is taken to fix an issue?
- How much time, on average, an issue is in the open state?
- How many long living issues are there in the system?

This sort of trend tracking helps us to improve our process for both, the current and future projects.

Another aspect related to the bug tracking system is the potential friction that can arise between parties due to bugs that are being raised. This is because of the kind of perspective that people will have towards the bugs that are being raised. The test team will raise bugs, and to do that, they need to use the system in anger. If they do not, they will not be effective in their job. However, the developers should not see those issues as fault-finding missions by the test team. Rather, the developers should accept the existence of the bugs with open mind, and try, fix, and learn from them.

Issue tracking can be combined with source code control. This integration makes it possible to associate source code revisions with issue IDs. This helps us to keep track of what code changes were done to fix which issues.

Some of the popular issue tracking software includes Trac (http://trac.edgewall.org/), Bugzilla (http://www.bugzilla.org/) and JIRA (http://www.atlassian.com/software/jira/). You can find more information on various issue tracking systems on this Wikipedia page: http://en.wikipedia.org/wiki/Comparison_of_issue_tracking_systems.

Configuration management

In the initial stages of a software project, we will have a product that will be installed and run as one single unit. Over time, we might need to patch some PHP classes and libraries, install the system on multiple operating systems, and support older and newer versions of the software that we have developed.

Let us take a simple example. Say that we have three components in our system—the business logic component, the data processing component, and the user interface component. Initially, we will build these three components, integrate them together, and ship the product. After the release, we find that we have way too many bugs in the user interface component. Thus, we fix those and ship a new version of the product, but only the user interface component has changed. Now the new release has a different configuration than the previous release. Consider the following diagram:

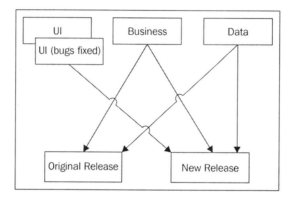

The Original Release and the New Release, as shown in the previous figure, are two different configurations of the software. The Original Release uses the user interface that was found to be buggy. The New Release has the user interface that includes bug fixes.

Managing multiple configurations is a problem that any decent software project needs to deal with. Even though the task might look simple in the initial iterations of a project, it can become a complex one over time if due attention is not given.

Configuration management can get very complicated and there are books written which are dedicated to the same. However, for our PHP projects, it is best to keep it simple and not complicate the matters. To deal with the matter in simple terms, we first need a basic understanding on why configuration management is required. Let's take an example to understand the need for configuration management.

Say, in an earlier iteration, we delivered some subset of functionality to the client. They are happy with the business logic, but want some user interfaces to be updated. Moreover, they want the user interface changes to be done immediately. Therefore, the team decides to do an upgrade of the user interface layer alone, on top of the business and data layers that have been delivered already. But the complication is that the team is already half way through to the new iteration, and they have improved the data, business logic, and the presentation layer to some extent. They can incorporate the changes requested into this new iteration's PHP code. However, it will not satisfy the timing requirement that the client has. Therefore, the best alternative is to update only the presentation PHP logic of the previous iteration's package. This essentially forces us to deal with the following three configurations:

- The original PHP code of the previous iteration
- The previous iteration's PHP code with presentation improvements
- The new iteration that is being worked on

Why do we need to keep track of all of these three configurations, given that the new iteration on which we are working is going to replace the older iterations? There are multiple reasons to keep track of these different configurations.

One key reason is to make sure that we will be able to recreate issues reported by the user as it is. If the users are using the second configuration and reported a bug against it, we might not be able to reproduce it in the latest iteration, once it is delivered. Either the bug might have been fixed or it can be the case that the issue is no longer applicable. This is because the improvements done in the latest iterations have wiped out the use case that caused the bug. If the bug was reported against the exact configuration along with the configuration information, the team members will be able to figure out the root causes with relative ease.

There can be other complications that arise due to the deployment scenarios. Say that the user runs the same system in multiple machines for some internal organizational reasons. Though this might not be the recommended scenario, it can often happen in reality. Moreover, when an upgraded presentation layer was given, they missed one of the deployments and did not upgrade it. Now when an issue is reported against the system that was not upgraded, the team will not be able to fix the issue, as they are being provided with wrong information. In such a situation, we need to have mechanisms, such as writing the configuration information to the log file, and ask the user to provide the log file of the system that caused the problem. This way, we can collect precise information on the configuration of the system that is in use.

Note that each developer's checking out on their machine is also some kind of deployment. Often, developers have a shared deployment that they use for internal testing. We need to allow the developers freedom to have their own deployment because they need to experiment and research when developing their part of the code, their own sandbox. However, we also need to ensure that the shared staging server always works with the contributions done by all of the members of the team from time to time. Moreover, when it comes to providing a snapshot to the client, we need to take the snapshot from the staging server. We can come up with a simple shell script to package a snapshot build on a regular basis and can get an automated set of tests, including system tests and unit tests to run on this pack to verify its integrity. Thus, we need to have some organized approach to make all of these deployments be in sync. Here is one way to achieve this. The developers work on their personal deployment. They will test all of the changes and upload those changes to the shared staging server, including the tests for those changes. The shared staging server runs with the changes contributed by all of the developers. A snapshot build is created out of the staging server and is tested with the tests contributed by the developers and is given to client for evaluation.

In order to record the configuration information in a log file, we need to have a systematic mechanism of specifying the configuration so that we know exactly which PHP code is running on the given system. The best way to be precise is to use a numbering system. The usual practice is to use version numbers with major, minor, and patch numbering.

Major version is incremented when major changes happen to the software package, which are not backward compatible. These changes include new features and improvements that were not a part of the previous release.

Minor version is incremented when there are changes and improvements, over the previous release, but there are no major new features. The changes are mainly limited to the enhancements of the previous features. Patch version is updated if the changes are restricted to bug fixes alone.

From the previous example, where we had three configurations of the previous iteration to current iteration, there needs to be a major version increment. For example, if the previous iteration was 1.0.0, the current iteration should be 2.0.0. When the presentation improvements are done to 1.0.0, it is a minor version increment so that configuration is version 1.1.0. Once 1.1.0 is delivered, if the users happen to find few issues, and if they requested to fix those immediately, as we are still busy with 2.0.0, we will fix the issues on 1.1.0 PHP code branch and release a 1.1.1.

The important aspect of configuration management with respect to collaboration is that when communicating with each other on issues, new features, improvements, and so on, we can use the version number to make sure that we precisely inform the other party which configuration we are talking about. This will prevent miscommunication and improve understanding between collaborating parties. The version number tells an entire story about the configuration in use and is a good example of shorthand jargon for explaining complex scenarios. For example, it is so precise when someone says, 'Feature Foo is broken in version 2.1.3', and everyone is clear about what exactly the PHP source bug is.

Sometimes, code names are used to describe configurations. This is because it is easier to remember a name, rather than numbers. However, note that the code name is not an alternative, version number is. Code name just complements the version number. Irrespective of the fact whether a code name is used or not, the version number must be used.

It is not sufficient to use the version number to refer to configurations by the development team alone. We must encourage all of the stakeholders to use configuration information in all of their communication, especially the users.

When the users raise bugs, they must use the configuration information and mention the bug that is being raised in the issue tracking system. Thus, bug reporting has a close relationship to configuration management.

Configuration management also relates to the source control that we discussed earlier in this chapter. When we create a branch off the source trunk of the PHP code base, we can use the version number to indicate which configuration the branch relates to. This way, anyone can very easily locate all of the entire PHP code that is related to a given configuration. At the point of release, we can use the configuration version number to name the tag. This ensures that we are conscious about the configuration that we are going to release. At this point, as well as at the point at which we are branching, we can question the version number based on the changes that goes into a release, and decide the right number that indicates the configuration.

Apart from the PHP source code libraries, components, or PHP classes, the deployment information can also have an impact on the configuration. For example, whether the source code is deployed on Linux or Microsoft Windows, if the web server being used is Apache httpd or Microsoft IIS, or if the database being used is MySQL, Oracle, or MS SQL Server, it will be important configuration information that will be useful when figuring out root causes of issues and meeting security or performance aspirations. If the development team uses one deployment configuration, the test team another, and the client yet another, then that will not help when trying to replicate the issues that are being reported. Therefore, at least the test team should have the exact client deployment scenario replicated in-house so that they will see the problems before the users do. The developers can use the test team's deployment setup to help replicate issues while fixing them.

Having the configuration information only in the source control system or the issue tracking system will not help in managing the configuration information in the long run. We should at least maintain a simple spreadsheet to capture the following information:

- On what configurations was it done
- On which date was it done
- If we have more than one client, then for which client was it done

Tools for communication and collaboration

We can use various means for the collaboration of a wide array of channels for communicating. The best is to use a collection of tools to facilitate robust and effective communication. At the same time, it must be clear where to find the specific information by avoiding redundancy among the set of tools. For example, we can use a mailing list for discussion and each discussion will need to have a resulting change on a shared web page, such as a Wiki page that summarizes the decisions made. Without such guidelines, it will take more time to find the necessary information among many channels available and some of the team members will work with non up-to-date information.

One of the earliest and most effective channels of communication is email. Research teams, developers, users, and many other groups have used email for many years and it has proven to work for many purposes. Rather than one to one emails, or copying several people in the email, the best way to use email is to set up some lists. We can have multiple lists for various purposes. For example, consider the following:

- **Developer list**: Includes all of the team members
- **User list**: Includes all users and developers
- **Customer list**: Includes all of the key stakeholders' from the customer's end, and the project and organizational leader's from the software organization.
- **Leadership list**: Includes project leadership

From these, as far as the project's success is concerned, the most important lists are the Developer list and the User list.

Developers can use the Developer list to discuss matters, such as design, PHP code, PHP libraries, coding patterns, bugs, and so on.

Users can use the User list to provide feedback, ask questions, voice their opinions, and get help from the developers. Since all of the developers are also on the user list, users can get all of the help they want form the developers. The User list can set the platform for the developers and users to collaborate and build a relationship with each other.

Use of mailing lists can get tough for some situations, especially when there are negotiations required, or when some things need to be done fast. Email, as a communication channel, has some time lag associated with it. Especially given the fact that the subscribers or recipients will respond to the mails when they feel like it or when they have some time.

To make it real time, as opposed to asynchronous, as in the case of email, we can use instant messaging. Moreover, as in the case of email, rather than doing one to one chats, we can use chat rooms. We can use multiple chat rooms for various groups, one for developers and one for users with the developers also participating.

The benefit of chat rooms is the fact that they are real time and there is no time lag to get a response, provided the people are available. But that can also cause problems. When the developers are busy, and if the users keep on bugging them in the chat room all of the time, it will hinder productivity.

If there are urgent matters that need to be discussed, and decisions that are to be made, then neither chat nor email will help. If it is about resolving some conflicting views on a design, then it will be hard to get all of the team members to agree on something. This is because email threads can go astray and chat rooms can fill with noise. The best channels for such scenarios would be to have face-to-face meetings or a conference call. A call or a meeting is real time, more humane, and helps to reach decisions on the spot, given that the team stays focused.

When it comes to meetings or calls, sticking to the original purpose and staying focused is very important. The best way is to define the length of the meeting at the start and finish within that slot.

With the advent of Web 2.0, there are an array of new tools that can be used to facilitate communication and collaboration. The so called social media provides some powerful platforms and tools for effective communication.

One of the first Web 2.0 style tools that has been widely adopted is the concept of Wiki. The idea is to have a collection of web pages that can be edited with the team by using a simpler set of syntax to formulate documents. The advantage is that not only can those documents be found easily, but they can also be edited easily to correct mistakes. Thus, they add improvements on the fly. For the PHP team, Wikis can be useful for the following reasons:

- **Design documents**: We can maintain a single page on which all of the design related documents, such as how the data model and business model are linked. Those who want to find them just need to come to this Wiki page.

- **Coding conventions**: We can document PHP coding styles that are used for the project in a Wiki and we can improve that as and when needed.

- **Process information**: Team members need to find information about the process from time to time. They should be directed to a central page with all of the process information, and that should link to other Wiki pages that have all of the process information. Also, when the process needs improvements, the Wiki provides the means to update it with ease to meet the process' fine tuning needs of the team.

- **Best practices**: PHP coding best practices can be documented using Wikis and fine tuned with the teams' experiences over time.

- **Configuration information**: A Wiki is a good tool to maintain PHP source configuration information. It helps to keep all of the configuration management related information online. Thus, it helps to make sure that the team will have that information at their fingertips when they are attending issues.

- **Test plans**: Having test plans on a Wiki serves multiple purposes. First, it helps anyone to locate what the plan is, and second, it allows adding, modifying, and improving the test plans regularly. In addition to test plans, we can also keep track of all PHP test cases, where they are stored, and how to run them.

- **Guidelines**: Various guidelines instructing the team on how to approach certain tasks can also be documented with Wikis.

Any PHP project's team need to evolve with time. Not only does the team needs to be agile, but also, the team needs to have access to agile tools to enable them to be on that path. The ability to be edited on the fly and update, improve, and upgrade the content is a great asset of Wikis that enables agility. One may worry that such an easy approach to edit and change content will lead to chaos. However, as we discussed in the chapter on agile principles, when the team becomes really agile, they also become self-organized. You can entrust such a team to do the right thing. Therefore, it is not a problem, but rather an asset, to have the free edit capability in Wiki.

Wiki sites can be used to capture a wealth of knowledge and can serve as a very useful and powerful knowledge base for the project's team. It is good practice to keep the content organized. The Wiki can contribute to the betterment of the informative workspace. All of the information required in making decisions, finalizing designs, carrying our testing, verifying code quality, and review activities are supported by the knowledge captured in the Wiki pages.

Most Wiki software supports automatic versioning. Therefore, if the need arises to go back to a previous version of a document, or have a peek at the older content to verify against new content, then that would be facilitated.

When someone asks for information on a mailing list, if that is already captured in Wiki, then the one with a question can be pointed there. If multiple users keep on asking the same question repeatedly, then that can be documented in the Wiki and the users can be pointed there. This saves time and energy on the part of the developers, as opposed to repeat the same answer over and over again.

Most of the Wiki software also comes with a search facility, so over time, developers and users will get used to search in Wiki before asking others.

Wikis can be thought of as a means for achieving shared content management. Therefore, it can be used to write all sorts of documentation, including user-oriented documentation. If we also allow users to edit the pages, then users can contribute to the betterment of documentation by fixing trivial typos that they tend to find.

Forums have been around for a while now. It seems that even though email has been there for a long time, and has been used by teams effectively for a long time, the new generation of computer users prefer forums to email. This is also partly due to the popularity of Web 2.0 style applications, such as Facebook.

Forums are quite similar to email lists in nature, that is, they too are asynchronous and the subscriber can choose to have a look at it when they have time or when they feel like. We can have a number of forums for various groups, such as developer's forum and user's forum.

The differences between email lists and forums include the fact that forums are online with web-based interfaces. Readers will need to visit those pages to gather the latest information. On the contrary, mailing lists deliver the messages to subscribers' mailing inbox. While you need to make an effort and visit the forum, the mail is in the inbox and you can see that while checking on other emails.

White boards are very powerful tools, even in this Web 2.0 era. Unlike the case of the constrained space on a computer screen, the white board in the center of a team meeting can be very robust and powerful tool. Though it is two dimensional, when combined with enthusiastic and energetic team, no other tool might be able to match the power of a white board.

The white board helps us to keep things simple, yet very effective. The simple diagrams, charts, and bullet points that are captured with a pen on the white board can be photographed and stored as they are in a Wiki. They can serve as the design documentation and historic records of various discussions. The central place used to store white board images can serve as another form of PHP team's knowledge base.

Tracking tools

Project visibility is an important aspect. Every stakeholder of the PHP project will be interested in knowing what is going on with the project. We can use various tools to track the progress of the project.

Earlier, we discussed the use of an issue tracking system to capture bugs in the system. Many issue tracking tools also come with the facility to track the project's progress. In other words, issue tracking systems support some elements of project's management. Not only bugs, but also the new features could create issues and then can be associated with a version. This way, we can associate the state life cycle that is used to track the issue's progress with all new features, gauge the progress, and predict if we will be able to deliver it in time for the next release iteration.

There are various other tools available to help with time tracking and progress tracking. Those tools can help a team to see if they are on track for the next iteration deliveries. When initial estimates are compared with the actual time spent, we can also measure our ability to estimate a task precisely.

Even though we might be able to deal with estimates that are off the mark for some time, in the long run, both, the development team as well as the clients and users will become frustrated with incorrect estimates, especially underestimates. The usual trend is to underestimate time because humans are usually over confident about their skills. When the clients become increasingly frustrated with the constant delays in delivery, and express that to the team then the team, will go on the defense. When defensive, they will always over estimate the time required with some unreasonable buffers. That too will frustrate clients, as they will always want the product sooner.

Tracking tools will ensure that we become more realistic about our estimates. This is because we will know for real, how much time it really took to do a task, with time tracking in place. We can use that experience next time around for estimating the efforts required to complete a given task. This does not mean that it will make our estimates precise over time, but it means we will come close to reality with our estimates, more often than not.

Sometimes, tracking tools can be seen as a means to micro management because the project and organizational leadership can drill down the details of how each individual works. But that should not be the correct attitude when looking into the use of tracking tools for the project. It should be understood that these tools are for the betterment of the project and the project's team. For example, if one person does something sooner than the other, there will be some productivity tips to learn form the team member who did it faster. If a member seems to get the estimated numbers right, which would reflect form the tracking system, we would be able to ask him to teach others the secret of success.

Summary

This chapter was dedicated to the topic of communication and collaboration. The PHP project is about delivering high quality PHP code that works. Note that it is not just the PHP code. The phrase 'that works' is very important. That is, the PHP code needs to work within the expectations of the users.

To make sure that the software we develop is 'working software', we need to collaborate very closely with all of the stakeholders. The developer-user collaboration is the key and is the most important. The developer-developer collaboration is also important for the project's success.

There are various channels to facilitate collaboration that can bring great benefits when used appropriately. Emails, instant messaging, conference calls, and face-to-face communication are some of those channels. Web 2.0 technologies also add a lot of other channels, including forums, Wiki pages, and social networking sites.

Source control, bug tracking, and configuration management are interdependent activities that, if done right, will contribute to the success of the project by a great deal.

Time tracking tools, and historical data that is collected through them, can help to increase project visibility and predictability. Thus, the chance of a project's success increases. More than egos or concerns over micro-management possibilities, the team needs to focus on the potential to succeed with tracking tools.

The channels and tools are of no use if the team members and users do not make effective use of them. It is up to the developers and users to make the best use of them and be effective to ensure project's success. Rather than trying to define rules to govern how to use the channels, let the team use the channels and figure out the best use for each one over time.

7
Continuous Improvement

Change is inevitable. No matter how hard we try, we will not be able to live without changing the PHP code that we have already written. Sometimes it will come in the form of enhancements, improvements, or new features requested by users. Other changes will come from bugs in the system. No matter how perfect the design or the PHP code is, we will need to face these change requests and we will need to change the code.

Change should be embraced with positive attitude and should be treated as an opportunity for evolution. No system, be it written in PHP or any other programming language, would ever be perfect. Therefore, there is always room for improvement. The idea is not to keep on improving the PHP code in an infinite loop, rather, it is to improve as and when the need arises. Moreover, by design, the system needs to support the change.

Whenever you change a piece of software that is working, it might break. No matter how experienced the PHP developer is, the chances of him breaking something in the system due to a change is real. This is why it is said that working software should not even be touched. On one hand, changes must be done. On the other hand, changes pose the risk of breaking the system. Therefore, we need to devise mechanisms to facilitate the change without breaking the system.

Plans don't always work, but we ought to keep on planning. We might have well defined and well documented processes and procedures within the organization. However, if those plans are inflexible, we will not progress at all. This also applies to the PHP software project on which we are working. In order to make sure we achieve successful completion of the project, not only should we have a process, but we should also be willing to adjust, change, and adopt the process at any stage of the project. In other words, we should continuously improve along the way.

In order to achieve continuous improvement, we need to know the following few things regarding our PHP project:

- Where are we?
- Where are we going?
- Where do we want to go?

In order to answer these questions, we need to have data about the PHP project on which we are working. For data collection, we need to measure the outcomes of the projects and the PHP system that is being developed. This will help us to make informed decisions on the process.

In this chapter, we will be discussing the following:

- Dealing with change in PHP applications
- Ensuring that the change process is effective
- Evolving the PHP application
- People development
- Ensuring success with teams

Dealing with change in PHP applications

As it is not possible to live without a change, the smart approach to deal with the change is to design the system with room for change. For example, in the PHP application, the template based approach for designing the presentation layer will facilitate future changes of the user interface with minimal effort. The PHP framework that we choose has a lot of say here. If the PHP framework allows us to maintain and manage all of the templates with minimal effort and in a systematic manner, then we will have little to worry about serving the user change requests. The presentation layer is only one example. The data layer and the business logic layer can also be subjected to change.

Facilitating the change is a mindset, more than a technical issue. If the team members are reluctant to change the PHP code, then it is hard to facilitate the change. Also, the developers need to keep in mind the need for change. That way, they will seek for the features in the framework and use tools that will help themselves in designing the system for the change.

Simple techniques, such as declaring constants, rather than hardcoding the values into the PHP code, abstracting out the logic into functions, classes, and components, and leaving a room for alternate logic when implementing the PHP code can also facilitate the ease of change at the PHP code level. For example, let's take a constant string value. At first, it might seem as if there is only one use of the string and we can have the value used in the code logic segment itself. Over time, as the system evolves, the number of uses for the string can increase. Let's say the string represents a URL and the URL changes. We might now need to change all references to the string in the code. If we used a constant, instead of hard coding the value everywhere, we just need to make a change in one place. The same applies to the logic segments that can be implemented using the same code. When we want to upgrade the functionality, we need to apply the change in multiple places. If we encapsulate the common logic segments into a function and call that function, then it becomes simple to upgrade the logic, as there is only one place to change.

One technique that can be useful when designing the system with future changes in mind is to evolve the system as the project progresses, rather than trying to implement the complete solution in one go. This is the advantage of using an iterative approach to the delivery of the system. Implement some useful functionality, deliver it to the user, collect feedback, and then improve it based on the feedback. Improvements done to satisfy the users' feedback evolves the system to the next level and changes the system for its betterment. This is one of the reasons why the agile process encourages collaborating closely with the users. We discussed the agile principles in Chapter 5, *Agile Works Best*, of this book.

Evolution of the system should be stepwise, rather than big-bang. Big-bang evolution is not sustainable and destroys ecosystems. Therefore, first, the team members need to be made aware of the phase and scale of the changes that they are doing, and then break them into smaller chunks. Breaking changes into smaller chunks helps to ensure that we do not break the system while evolving.

Doing changes in smaller chunks alone will not ensure a stable system state after the change. We also need a system, a set of tools to ensure that we do the right changes, so that we are not breaking the system. As discussed in the previous chapter, the best tool that we can use to prevent instability after a change is a test framework. All tests in the framework should pass, both before and after the change. This is the best known technique to prevent regression issues.

If the change in the PHP code results in a behavior change that also requires one or more existing tests to be updated, then the tests also need to be changed. Thus, system integrity is ensured. Also note that some changes will require new tests to be written. This is to make sure that the integrity of the current feature improves against the future changes.

Test-based verification of integrity is a welcome habit to be developed by all team members in the PHP team. The trivial nature of the PHP code changes should not be taken for granted, and running the test framework should not be skipped at any time. If one does, it could be hard to locate the point at which the system started breaking. This especially applies to situations where the code is shared through a source control system.

Backward compatibility is another key concern in the evolution of the PHP product. When changes are done, we need to ensure that previous versions that are delivered through the previous iteration of the project are not drastically different form the latest version. There are various implications in being backward compatible. One is that the user interface of the evolved system should not have a drastic face lift from the previous version. This is because the users are already familiar with the older interface. If the changes are very drastic, such as the form submission button that used to be on the left bottom is now on the right bottom, the users will take a considerable amount of time to adapt. Sometimes, changes are so large that we might not even imagine learning and getting used to it. This is the presentation aspect of being backward compatible. One might call this being consistent with respect to the user interface. The data layer and the business logic layer needs to keep to the backward compatibility principle. For example, if an API is changed, it is advisable not to delete the older API right away. Instead, mark it to be deprecated first and then make it obsolete in a future release and not the current release. You can either use a warning level log message or a console message to warn against the use of a deprecated API call. In addition to these warning messages, it must also be documented in the PHP code so that anyone referring to the API code or the API documents would notice.

Ensuring process effectiveness

In Chapter 4, *The Process Matters*, we discussed the need for a process. While having a process is important, we also need to ensure that the process fits the project on which we are working, and is effective. The process should help people to write quality code, be productive with the work, and encourage collaboration.

Knowing how we are doing is important before we try and improve the process. The best way to get to know about how it is doing is to have some measurements on the process and the product. There are numerous measurements that we can make on the process and the outcome of the process, which is the product. Some possible things that we can measure are as follows:

- The number of PHP classes in the system
- The number of PHP functions
- The number of presentation layer pages

- The number of forms and reports
- The number of PHP classes or functions that are added per day, week, or month
- The number of presentation forms, reports that are added per day, week, or month
- The number of PHP classes or functions that are written by a developer per day, week, or month
- The number of bugs that are raised per day, week, or month
- The number of bugs being fixed per day, week, or month
- The number of PHP code that commit messages to the source code repository per day, week, or month
- The number of emails or forum messages sent that are posted per day, week, or month by developers or users
- The number of visits made to the Documentation Wiki per day, week, or month

Measurements alone will not drive us towards any progress. Measured data needs to be analyzed, and information should be extracted and actions should be taken based on the outcomes of the analysis. Also, it is important to correlate the related measurements to extract the real meaning of the data and the implications of those on the PHP project.

For example, the greater the number of issues that are being fixed per day portrays a good picture on the performance of the PHP team. However, we also need to take into account the number of issues being raised per day. If the rate of opening bugs and resolving those bugs are parallel, then we do not have an issue. However, if the issue's open rate is much higher than the issue's fix rate, then it requires further investigation, as to what is going on.

Some simple measurement, such as the number of visits to the Documentation Wiki, can reveal a wealth of information on the quality of the project. For example, if the visits to the API documentation are high, then that indicates the PHP developers do make use of API calls written by others. Fewer number of visits would indicate that the other developers are not using that API. No matter how expert or how smart the team members are, it is not easy to remember all API calls. Thus, if they are really using it, they will need to refer to the API documentation. However, the team members who are always visiting the API documentation may also mean that the API is not designed properly. It is at the beginning of the use of an API that a newbie to the API needs to refer to the documents. When the user of the API becomes familiar with it, it becomes intuitive to use without spending much time on reading the documents. Therefore, the evaluation of the number of visits to the documents needs to be combined with context and realities on the ground to depict the real meaning.

If we keep on adding new features, that would mean that the PHP code cannot be made stable. We can use the number of code changes done in a particular period of time to help determine the active development patterns. Nearing a release of the number of commits has to go down as the PHP code gets stabilized. But in the early stage of iteration, there should be lots of code changes going on. If we have the reverse pattern, that would mean we are not doing a good job with the release management. If we have lots of commits towards the latter part of the project iteration, the chances of missing the deadline is higher, as it takes time for changes to stabilize. Over time, if we repeatedly see that we require some sleepless nights, and if we double or triple the regular efforts towards the end of the iteration, then it would be time to fix the formation of our process.

It would also be useful to talk to team members to figure out how they feel about the process. The PHP team themselves can provide an insight as to how effective the process is, and what elements of the process help them and what hinders them. Team satisfaction towards the process in use can be highly subjective. Yet it is an important aspect that determines the success of the project.

If the PHP team members are repeatedly skipping a step in the process, or do not adhere completely to the guidelines set fourth, that is an indication of the ineffective procedures. We must take steps to improve those in the process, or else, after some time, we will either be left without a proper process, or will end up with an ad hoc set of steps to write and debug the PHP code.

Developer feedback and the metrics generated based on the data collected should help us to make informed decisions to enhance the process in use. The learning outcomes of the past iterations or past projects can be fed into the future iterations or projects. Therefore, process improvements should not be viewed as a single process exercise. As the way we use learning outcomes on PHP APIs and features from one project to another, we can use the project related learning outcomes across the projects on which we work.

Similar to the way in which users can provide useful feedback to the product that is being delivered, we can also get the users to help us improve the process, both directly and indirectly. On the fact whether we are able to deliver quality software or not, the bugs raised by users provide direct feedback on the process. More bugs being reported by the users means that the users are really using the system. It also means that the users want to get it fixed as they see the fixed system to be useful to them. If there are no bugs reported at all by the users, the chances are that the users are not really using the application that we have developed. Thus, we should try and figure out what is wrong by talking to the users.

The usage pattern for the PHP software that we develop also reveals useful information on the process, as the product quality is directly related to the process. The number of visits to the PHP-based site, the entry and exit patterns, the user error frequencies, and even the visitor timing patterns will reveal information on our project team capabilities. For example, the entry and exit patterns are related not only to our ability to design user interface flow effectively, but also to the effectiveness of our business logic flow design.

Ensure you are improving

Measuring is one thing. Taking steps to improve is another. Ensuring that we are really improving is yet another activity.

To start with, we need to measure, or else we cannot make informed decisions to improve the process we have. While taking steps to improve the process, we need to keep on measuring. The old data and the new data then need to be compared to ensure that the steps that we took with the intention of improving the process have really helped. If the steps have not helped towards improving, then we need to adjust again.

Fine-tuning and adjusting the process is an ongoing activity. In other words, we need to be doing continuous improvement to the process. In a previous chapter, we discussed the need for the process and the need for the process being agile. The agile process not only helps with delivering the product with quality, it also helps with process improvement. The self-organization of the team in affect means that they are improving the way they work. Over time, the process gets improved naturally with the agile process.

Evolving PHP applications

As we have discussed throughout this book, change is a must. As the project progresses, the gap between the user and the PHP team closes, and the application evolves from the first iteration to the last.

Not only will the user requirements change, but also the technologies, hardware, platforms, and programming techniques and paradigms will change and evolve. Even within a year, there can be a huge gap between what we used to do at the beginning of the year and what we would be doing at the end of the year with respect to technology. New technology hypes survive the mushroom factor, some of them survive while some do not. Irrespective of the survival factor, we might need to peruse them at a given point in time. The PHP team needs to be ready to live with that.

How can we ensure that new emerging technologies are incorporated into the application that we are building? Sometimes, it will be the right technology to use. Sometimes, it will not even make sense in the context of the project on which we are working. The options available to us are as follows:

- Use the current technology that we are familiar with, but which might also be an old technology

- Consider the state of the art technology, but with associated risks of unknowns and unexpected outcomes

It might be hard to tell at times if we should embrace the new technology or not. Thus, we might need to do some research and development, a quick proof of concept, or a feasibility study. To minimize the risk, we might use only one or two of the team members for evaluation while others focus on the regular activities. As an example, take the use of some **software as a service (SaaS)** elements in our application. We might want to evaluate it for some elements of our application, the SaaS model might work. We used to develop the PHP applications based on a database. In other words, our applications were data driven and we used them to manage our own data. However, the new trend is to make use of services that are made available by various service providers. Therefore, more than connecting to a database and pulling the data, all that we need to do is access the service provided by a third party and get our application done. Moreover, we can also become service providers to others. We used to call it **LAMP** or **WAMP** (Linux/Windows, Apache, MySQL, PHP) because the database was a part and parcel of the application. However, modern applications would use a smaller database and a set of services from the Internet to implement the application. Instead of being data driven, the application is now service oriented. The team needs to be willing to embrace these sorts of paradigm shifts, as that provides major business value to the application's users.

The framework that we are using right now might need to be updated in the next release of the PHP application. Based on the changes done into the framework, that could mean a major undertaking of application's evolution. Before upgrading to the latest version of the framework, we must evaluate if it is really necessary to go for a major framework upgrade of our application. If it is deemed that a framework upgrade is not really beneficial, we should not upgrade just for the sake of upgrading.

The set of PHP classes, the API, and the layouts of the presentation layer, will all be subjected to evolution. For example, the advances in the **Human-Computer Interaction (HCI)** technologies will demand us to improve our user interface designs to match them.

We might need to enhance the logging mechanisms used in the PHP application to match the business activity that is monitoring the needs of the client through the PHP application. This might be a new challenge, as none of the team members would have thought about this, as there was no need to think about it. This sort of an improvement in the application is a new version of the application. It is different from other features that we implement for the application as this needs to blend into the rest of the existing application (the whole of it). The best solution in case of other sorts of new features is to divide and conquer. First, we need a set of tests that ensure that embedding by logging into the existing code does not break other functionalities. Thus, we first need to build the tests. Then, we also need to look into other non-functional aspects, such as performance and security. With more logging, performance would drop, but that should not drop below the level where the user would feel that it is slow. Security cannot be compromised at any cost. Therefore, we might need a security audit after the evolution.

The client might have set forth security and performance aspirations at the beginning of the project. With the evolution taking place, both the client and the PHP team might forget to run the performance and security related tests on a regular basis. Regular application performance evaluation and security audits must be carried out on the application throughout the application's life cycle. These can be a part of the regular test framework, but they require specific attention after every iteration that evolves the application.

Understanding the needs of the enterprises with respect to application evolution is also important. Let's have a look at an example, using the latest security updates (applying security patches to libraries), techniques for achieving high performance (using clustering techniques), and making use of existing applications and services (using SOA principles and the cloud computing techniques). We cannot expect the client to peruse enterprise trends alone and provide us with all of the information we need. Sometimes, the client would not be aware of that and we might be able to provide the client with the insight that is based on our past experiences.

Tools are the other aspect that are subject to evolution. The IDEs, the template tools, the source code configuration tools, bug tracking tools, and even the PHP engine evolve over time. We need to move along with them as a team. On one hand, we will miss out on important features if we do not upgrade. On the other hand, the users also want to keep on upgrading. Some systems take ages to migrate. The best example is even after so many years of PHP 5, until recently, there was wide usage of PHP 4. But as a PHP team, we need to be willing to even support PHP 6.

Note that the evolution of our PHP application needs to be synced with the versioning strategy that we are using for our configuration management.

Any software system that does not evolve will die. This is because if the users see that the software system is not meeting their expectations, they will abandon its use. In order to keep supporting the user's expectations, the software system must keep evolving because with the changes in the real world, the user's expectations also keep on changing.

People development

People are the single most valuable resource in any software project. Moreover, it is the greatest contributing factor for the success of any software project.

Keeping the PHP developers in the team happy all of the time is tough, but it is a must. Sometimes, users can cause unhappiness. But we cannot model or manipulate users' behavior. The best alternative is to train the developers to live with the annoyances caused by the users. It is just a part of a developer's life.

Some of the team members do not want to do the same thing over and over again. The best approach to solve this problem is to make sure that we balance out research and development activities with regular development and bug fixing activities. It is a fact that the project cannot afford to have novel and exciting work all of the time. There will be tiring and boring activities. Balancing this less attractive work with more attractive work is the only way we can keep all PHP developers excited.

Quality assurance is a skill. It is often taken for granted that anyone can do it. However, that is far from correct. More importantly, the developers should have a quality eye assurance when evaluating the code that they are developing. This can be very useful when doing pair programming. The one without the keyboard (in the pair) should put on a QA hat and explore possible cases of failure from time to time.

It is important to keep the team members happy to make sure that we can make them a part of the active evolution. Most of the continuous improvement activities that make the project successful require the will on the part of each team member. Team members need to be willing to be subjected to change. It is a mindset.

To make sure that we help each individual to improve, we need to be straight and open with each team member. We need to show the shortcomings then and there. Also, we need to applaud and reward hard work. Sometimes, sloppy work on the part of developers can lead to a lot of work and it could be misinterpreted as hard work. For example, the person who creates ten bugs needs to work for longer hours than the one who creates just three bugs. Thus, before rewarding someone who works for longer hours late into the nights and sometimes into the weekends, we need to evaluate the real reason for those long hours.

Rewarding the wrong person due to misjudgment can lead real workers (who get the job done right) into dissatisfaction. It is more damaging to the project's team in the long run. Rather than hard work, we need to reward smart work and quality work.

Do not work hard, but smart.

Training is important. Training can be on technical matters and non-technical factors. Technical matters can be taken for granted and overlooked. Therefore, sometimes it is good to repeat some training sessions, especially for those who have joined new. Team members can choose to participate, as they wish. However, there are tons of resources available on the Web today, and some say you just need to Google. It is far more efficient and effective to have a trainer to train the team. We have the flexibility to customize the training to suite the specific needs of the team. Also, we can get expert team members to do the training.

Training on non-technical aspects, such as communication, collaboration, teamwork, leadership, time management, and productivity can help the team to improve the way they work. The need for training required by the team member should be picked up by observing the way they work and the way they adhere to the process. The problem areas need to be identified and training should be organized to solve those problems.

The frequency and timing of the training needs to be picked carefully as well. Too many training sessions too often, would take away the meaning of the training. Also, the team would see it as a trouble, rather than a help. The timing of the training is useful so that the training on a particular area is done when the team needs it the most. That way, the team's active and productive involvement in the training could be guaranteed and best results could be reaped form the training for the project's success.

Teams and success

Success is a habit. In this context, **success** would mean building software according to the client's needs. The team needs to be successful in all of the projects, not in one, not in a couple. In other words, there should not be any failures at all, and it can be done.

The passion for success is built over time. With the techniques, such as agile methodology, tools, and technologies of today, we always have room to find steps for improvement.

Successful teams bond together over time. It has its pros and cons. On the positive side, we have a very good understanding among the team members. Self-organization has taken place and there should not be any barriers for collaboration. On the negative side, the high level of team bonding might lead to high barriers for entry of new people into the team. Team members would expect the same level of performance from new members and might not be willing to allow time for the new member to settle in and stabilize. One reason for this is the lack of understanding on the amount of time required for a team to self-organize, as the current team is not aware of the time it has taken.

Eliminating politics among the team members is also important. Over a period of time, groups can be created unconsciously among team members, and the power groups and powerhouses might form within the team. They will influence decisions, and they will deviate from the objectives and processes in place. This is not good for the team's health. All that is required is to have good rapport and good communication. Beyond that, unhealthy politics should not take place.

Over time, inertia builds within the team and it makes the team harder to move. Team inertia makes it hard for the team to evolve. One of the effects of agile methodology is to break up this inertia and make the team agile and open to change.

Simplicity is an art. It is tempting to go after elaborate designs, and think and argue about what is right and wrong. But from the user's perspective, the most important thing is to get something working and get it improved step by step. Therefore, keep it simple and make it usable. Do not ever try to come up with the perfect design in the first iteration.

Managing the team

To ensure that the team heads where they are supposed to, there needs to be someone who keeps the head straight and continues to look forward. Managing people is one of the most challenging tasks. Moreover, it is harder to manage educated people, such as software developers.

It is important to have a set of people who are trustworthy in a team. At the same time, trustworthy does not mean that they agree to all of the others at all times. It might seem that it is hard to manage a team with members that have different opinions. But at the same time, different opinions can expose the team to better alternatives. Therefore, it is good to have members on a team that seem to be hard to manage, but at the same time explore the world and bring the findings into the team.

Managing a PHP team does not require one to sit in a glass room and pull hair all day long. Chapter 5, *Agile Works Best*, mentioned what is required to move the team along and work with the team.

Every project has a clear end goal, which is delivering a quality product on time. The team needs to stay focused on this end goal. Moreover, it is the responsibility of the team management to make sure that this focus is kept throughout the project, among team members.

We allocate tasks to each member based on their skill sets. However, we cannot always guarantee that we can create an exact match of skill set and the assigned tasks. Therefore, we should make sure that the members are comfortable with the task allocation, and that we help them to expand their skill set to meet the challenges.

It is a fact that various team members run into technical problems throughout the project's life cycle. Problems often get worse, not because the problems are complex, but because team members do not raise the problems soon enough. The team management must keep all of the communication and collaboration paths open to encourage timely escalation of problems by team members. Every team member needs to be educated on the importance of escalation. Sometimes, some members need to be probed for problems because it will take some time for them to figure out on their own that there is a problem. We can make use of techniques, such as stand-up meetings that we discussed in Chapter 5, *Agile Works Best*.

Team interaction is also important for successful team management. We discussed this in detail in Chapter 6, *Ways of Collaboration*.

Conflicts are inevitable and need to be dealt with in the team's management. While having members with different ideas is beneficial, it can also lead to conflicts. The guiding principle to be used here is that everyone needs to stay focused on the project's success. If the conflict is about what the right technology is, use objective analysis to evaluate the impact of the conflicting alternatives on the project. If the conflict is about subjective ideologies, the parties involved need to be educated to focus on the project goals, rather than trying to delay the success of the project. However, while the key message is simple and straightforward, some delicate means, such as friendly face-to-face chat, must be used to convey this message to the parties involved in resolving conflicts.

Leadership

We need leaders all of the time. We can build leaders through delegation and can identify the real leaders in the process. Some people love to take responsibility, while others are happy in focusing on what they are doing, rather than worrying about the big picture. For those who want more ownership, it is best to give them a chance to lead based on their skill set and willingness.

Meritocracy is a very good model to follow when identifying leaders. Reward those who do valuable work. For this, we need to be able to identify the people who work smart and get the job done. We can make use of metrics that we discussed earlier to pick the smart workers. Moreover, we can combine those with the leadership skills that they exhibit in guiding people around them to get the job done. If a person worries about the overall project's direction, rather than just implementing his or her part of the code, then that is a clear sign of someone who has the capacity to lead. A leader should see the big picture, understand it, and direct others towards the end goals.

Some people emerge as leaders. They can get the team to achieve the project goals. They drive others to achieve success. Rather than appointing someone to be the leader, it would be useful to let these charismatic leaders guide the project towards success. However, when it comes to situations where decisions need to be made, having no clear point (as to whom to turn towards), would lead to chaos. Therefore, there must be some appointed person with leadership authority to make decisions and make the team move ahead when things are not flowing smoothly.

Quality focus

Elegant code, good documentation, bug free code, and simple design should be encouraged all of the time. No one should think that quality is someone else's responsibility. Quality is every team member's responsibility.

Constant monitoring

While discussing the agile process, we discussed the need for daily stand up meetings. They basically help us to monitor what is happening with the project on a daily basis. Carefully monitoring the needs of team members is quite critical to the project's success.

Being sensitive to what each team member is going through all of the time is very important. Sometimes, they might need some helping hand, or sometimes they just might need some time.

The team is human

It is very important to remember that the team is a group of human beings. It is a must that they enjoy their work. It is a must that they relax. It is a must that they achieve their expectations from life. The software project is not the only thing in their lives.

Summary

In this chapter, we discussed the need for continuous improvement in process, product, and the people involved.

Knowing what we are doing, where we are heading, and where we should be heading is very important for a software project. Metrics and measurements can help us to evaluate our current situation and figure out what is to be done in order to improve it. We can evolve the process that we use over time to have greater effectiveness to deliver quality products. Nurturing people and helping them to evolve is also critical because that helps both, the individuals and the team, a great deal over time.

Index

B

best practices
  enforcing 54, 55
bug control 131
bug issues, classifying
  new feature or improvement 134
  real bug 134
  use error 134
bug, PHP project
  Bugzilla, URL, 135
  controlling, 130
  issue tracking software, 135
  issue tracking system, 135
  issue tracking system, in Wikipedia, 135
  issues, 131
  issues, classifying, 134
  JIRA, URL, 135
  status, 132
  TODO note, writing in code, 130
  Trac, URL, 135
  tracking system, 134
  tracking system, need for, 130-132
  trend tracking, 135
bugs 82
bug, status
  Closed 132
  In-Progress 132
  Open 132
  Priority 133
  Resolved 132
  Severity 133
bug tracking system
  about 132
bug tracking, tools
  Bugzilla 25
  Jira 25
Bugzilla, issue tracking software
  URL 135
Bugzilla
  URL 25
business layer
  designs 89, 90
  implementing 90
business logic layer
  about 33
  aspects 41

complexity 41
business modelling 87, 88

C

CakePHP 67
Code Bits section 65
CodeIgniter 67
Coding by Convention 55
coding standards 54
collaboration
  ways 140
communication, tools
  about 25, 26
  calls, benefits 142
  chat rooms, benefits 141
  customer list 141
  developer list 141
  email 141
  email lists and forums, differences 144
  forums, benefits 144
  instant messaging, benefits 141
  leadership list 141
  mailing lists 141
  meetings, benefits 142
  user list 141
  white board, benefits 144
  Wiki 142
  Wiki, benefits 142, 143
community 57, 58
complexity
  versus number of team members 38
configuration management, PHP project
  about 139, 140
  example 136
  major version 138
  minor version 138
  need for 137
  patch version 138
  types 137
continous builds, tools 23, 24
continous integration 18, 19
controller
  about 20, 32
  business logic layer 33
Convention over Configuration 55

D

data layer
  about 33
  complexity 42
  designs 88
  implementing 89
data modelling 86, 87
design pattern. *See* also software design
        patterns
design pattern
  about 30
  benefits 30
  documentation elements 30
developers, issues
  Overworking 101
  product, inferior quality 100
  project completion, delay 101
  wrong product, producing 100
divide and conquer
  integration, guaranteeing 15
  patterns 14
  regression, preventing 15
  reuse, guaranteeing 14
documentation, PHP framework 56
Drupal
  URL 7
DSDM, agile process models
  about 111
  lifecycle 112
  Pareto principle used 111
DSDM, lifecycle
  business study 112
  feasibility study 112
  functional model iteration 112
  implementation 112
  iteration, building 112
  iteration, designing 112
Dynamic Systems Development Method.
        See DSDM, agile process models

E

Extreme Programming. *See* XP

F

Facebook
  URL 7
FDD, agile process models 114
Feature Driven Development. *See* FDD,
        agile process models
Flickr
  URL 7
Focus groups, AD 111
framework. *See* also PHP framework
framework
  expectations 49
  features 46-48
  team success 62, 64
  technical feasibility 64
functional API
  versus object oriented API 53

G

GIT
  URL 22

H

HCI 154
horizontal
  versus vertical division 15-17
Human-Computer Interaction. *See* HCI

I

integration
  making work 126, 127
integration challenges 42
intellectual property implications. *See* IP
        implications
internationalization, PHP framework 56
IP implications 61
issue tracking system, bug 135
issue tracking, tools 24, 25

J

Jira, isuue tracking software
  URL 135
Jira
  URL 25
Joomla
  URL 7

K

Keep it Short and Simple. *See* KISS
Keep it Simple, Stupid. *See* KISS
KISS
  about 69
  change, embracing 70, 71
  innovation 70
  Not Invented Here (NIH), avoiding 70
  simplicity 71

L

LAMP 154
Limb 65
loadTeenagers() function 34

M

macro package 65
Mission driven, AD 111
model
  about 20, 32
  data layer 33
MVC
  about 31
  controller 32
  dealing, with change 34-37
  helping, ways 33, 34
  intent 31
  library system, example 34, 35
  mapping, into real implementation 34
  model 32
  motivation 31
  solution 32
  view 32

MVC, implementing with team
  about 38
  presentation layer (view), aspects 38-40
  team distribution 42
MVC Pattern. *See* MVC

N

NIH
  avoiding 70
Not Invented Here. *See* NIH
number of team members
  versus complexity 38

O

object oriented API
  versus functional API 53
Object-Oriented Programming. *See* OOP
Object Relational Mapping. *See* ORM
OOP 14
ORM 62

P

Pareto principle 111
patterns
  as solutions 19, 20
PDO 42
people, PHP project
  development 156
PHP
  about 7
  process effectiveness, ensuring 153
  process effectiveness, measuring 150-152
PHP applications
  changes, dealing with 148-150
  evolving 153-155
  improving, need for 36
PHP code
  changes, need for 147
PHP Data Objects. *See* PDO
phpDrone 65
PHP framework
  about 65, 148
  Akelos 66, 67

U

UI 83
user activity
  analysis 88
user interface
  implementations 91, 92
User Interface. *See* UI

V

vertical
  versus horizontal division 15-17
view
  about 20, 32
  presentataion layer 33

W

WAMP 154
web_app package 65
Web Programming 8
WordPress
  URL 7

X

XP
  coding 108
  design 107
  planning 107
  testing 109
XP coding 108
XP design 107
XP planning 107
XP testing 109

Z

Zend Framework 67, 68
ZNF 66

Thank you for buying
PHP Team Development

Packt Open Source Project Royalties

When we sell a book written on an Open Source project, we pay a royalty directly to that project. Therefore by purchasing PHP Team Development, Packt will have given some of the money received to the open source PHP project.

In the long term, we see ourselves and you—customers and readers of our books—as part of the Open Source ecosystem, providing sustainable revenue for the projects we publish on. Our aim at Packt is to establish publishing royalties as an essential part of the service and support a business model that sustains Open Source.

If you're working with an Open Source project that you would like us to publish on, and subsequently pay royalties to, please get in touch with us.

Writing for Packt

We welcome all inquiries from people who are interested in authoring. Book proposals should be sent to author@packtpub.com. If your book idea is still at an early stage and you would like to discuss it first before writing a formal book proposal, contact us; one of our commissioning editors will get in touch with you.

We're not just looking for published authors; if you have strong technical skills but no writing experience, our experienced editors can help you develop a writing career, or simply get some additional reward for your expertise.

About Packt Publishing

Packt, pronounced 'packed', published its first book "Mastering phpMyAdmin for Effective MySQL Management" in April 2004 and subsequently continued to specialize in publishing highly focused books on specific technologies and solutions.

Our books and publications share the experiences of your fellow IT professionals in adapting and customizing today's systems, applications, and frameworks. Our solution-based books give you the knowledge and power to customize the software and technologies you're using to get the job done. Packt books are more specific and less general than the IT books you have seen in the past. Our unique business model allows us to bring you more focused information, giving you more of what you need to know, and less of what you don't.

Packt is a modern, yet unique publishing company, which focuses on producing quality, cutting-edge books for communities of developers, administrators, and newbies alike. For more information, please visit our website: www.PacktPub.com.

Object-Oriented Programming with PHP5

ISBN: 978-1-847192-56-1   Paperback: 272 pages

Learn to leverage PHP5's OOP features to write manageable applications with ease

1. General OOP concepts explained

2. Implement Design Patterns in your applications and solve common OOP Problems

3. Take full advantage of native built-in objects

4. Test your code by writing unit tests with PHPUnit

Building Websites with PHP-Nuke

ISBN: 978-1-904811-05-3   Paperback: 320 pages

A practical guide to creating and maintaining your own community website with PHP-Nuke

1. Step through creating your own web portal with PHP-Nuke

2. Simple and practical guidance to mastering PHP-Nuke

3. For people with basic knowledge of web development

Please check **www.PacktPub.com** for information on our titles

LaVergne, TN USA
09 September 2009
157232LV00001B/43/P